OVERTHINKING

Discover Mindfulness for Creativity and Slow
Down Your Brain

(Build Mental Toughness and a Strong Mindset)

Jess Clark

I0095512

Published by Knowledge Icons

Jess Clark

Overthinking: Discover Mindfulness for Creativity and Slow Down Your Brain (Build Mental Toughness and a Strong Mindset)

ISBN 978-1-990084-67-6

Legal & Disclaimer

The information contained in this book is not designed to replace or take the place of any form of medicine or professional medical advice. The information in this book has been provided for educational and entertainment purposes only.

The information contained in this book has been compiled from sources deemed reliable, and it is accurate to the best of the Author's knowledge; however, the Author cannot guarantee its accuracy and validity and cannot be held liable for any errors or omissions. Changes are periodically made to this book. You must consult your doctor or get professional medical advice before using any of the suggested remedies, techniques, or information in this book.

Upon using the information contained in this book, you agree to hold harmless the Author from and against any damages, costs, and expenses, including any legal fees potentially resulting from the application of any of the information provided by this guide. This disclaimer applies to any damages or injury caused by the use and application, whether directly or indirectly, of any advice or information presented, whether for breach of contract, tort, negligence, personal injury, criminal intent, or under any other cause of action.

You agree to accept all risks of using the information presented inside this book. You need to consult a professional medical practitioner in order to ensure you are both able and healthy enough to participate in this program.

TABLE OF CONTENTS

Introduction

Overthinking (as the name implies) is excessive thinking about something, such as a subject, an issue, an event, or other matters, and what decisions to make regarding these subjects, issues, events, or other matters in the present or the future. Overthinking is not a behavior that only a few people exhibit; it happens to everyone in their daily lives. Maybe you have found yourself in a grocery store trying to select healthy food to purchase, spending way too long trying to decide which type of bread or tea that you would like to buy. Overthinking could also occur, for example, when we are playing a softball game, and our brain keeps planning, strategizing, and preparing when the ball has already been played by our opponent.

Some people experience constant overthinking; for others, this behavior occurs much less frequently. Research on overthinking has revealed that the brain constantly predicts the future and is always in anticipation of what will happen next. In a "Caveman Times" article, this behavior of the brain is compared to a caveman's prediction that a lion was probably following the heard of running antelopes, and he should stay away. But today, this can be compared to be mulling over the healthfulness of the meal items in a restaurant menu before selecting what to eat or drink. This could also mean carefully spending a lot of time considering the wording of a post to Facebook or Twitter while in fearful anticipation of harsh or critical judgment by the hundreds of followers and other people viewing the post.

Lori Hilt, Ph.D., an Assistant Professor of Psychology at Lawrence University in Wisconsin further explains that what happens to the brain when you over think is that you go round and round in a loop of repetitive thoughts when you ought to conclude on a course of action, move forward and solve the problem. While it is true that some degree of reflection helped us to survive and thrive in the past but too much also traps us in the realm of overthinking. Also, our past experiences and decisions are major contributors to our present overthinking behaviors.

Researchers have revealed that women tend to do more overthinking than men. At least about 42 percent of women excessively think about subjects, issues or events as a result of being too attuned to emotions while trying hard to understand them. This research then suggested that environmental factors such as how one is raised could contribute to this and that, furthermore, overly-controlling parents could be the cause because such mothers and fathers constantly suppress the thoughts of their kids.

According to Hilt, "Overthinking means we spend most of our time in the past or the future". Hilt says it is very hard to be in the present moment because the mind is constantly racing. One example of living in the past is a veteran soldier who comes back from a long war; he may try to deal with the present people in his life based on his interactions with other people during his war experiences. He may have found these people to be unkind, brutal or wicked; however, the people in his present life may or may not possess those certain characteristics. This war experience may cause the veteran to always think obsessively about what type of behavior to expect from them, what they mean, how to deal with them, etc.

The anticipation of the future is a type of overthinking that a student who is about to prepare for an exam might experience; he keeps thinking about the short time he or she has to read, what questions will be asked, or in what the instructor or examiner will mark his or her answer. Should he/she look at past questions or example questions? Will the results of this exam help or hurt his/her final grade?

When, in reality, the best course of action for this student is to pick up the book and study.

Roy Baumeister, Ph.D., a research psychologist at Florida State University, who is also a co-author of the book called "Willpower", said that you tend to experience decision fatigue when you are trying to choose what to buy and not to buy, what to eat and what not to eat, or whether to go the gym or take a nap. All this lessens your self-control. He further makes his statement clear by adding that "you order a pizza because you are already overwhelmed to think about what to prepare for dinner, and it could be that you buy expensive appliances because you are worried out by making a comparison when shopping."

Domina Petric, MD, made it known that overthinking is a representation of a loop of unproductive thoughts. It is also considered to be an excessive amount of thoughts that are unnecessary. He further explained that overthinking can be linked to anxiety. In his approach to solve this overthinking disorder, he postulated that the entanglement of knots of negative emotions is expedient and should be replaced with positive knots of emotions.

Anxiety and depression can be the cause of negative emotions. In a situation where we can't find a balance between positive and negative emotions, negative emotions may take over. However, it is also important to realize that negative emotion is inevitable as it has its function in the balancing of healthy emotions. The ingredients of negative emotions are guilt, shame or disgrace, depression, despair, hopelessness, fear, worry, concern, nervous, irritation, frustration, annoyance, rage, panic, and more. These negative emotions happen naturally.

A person could be angered in a dangerous situation, and aggression has an important role to play by triggering the fast and efficient reaction to the dangerous situation; however, when the dangerous situation is gone, there is the need for positive emotion, such as gratitude, to balance the negative one. However, in a situation where such danger happens and is solved with anger or aggression, but there is no positive emotion to balance things, pathological anxiety and depression can occur. Knots of negative emotion lead to overthinking, and the mind can play a role in compensating this defection with intellectual overbalance.

Many factors lead to overthinking, such as excessive parental control, environmental factors during childhood, experience, emotional entanglement, and many more. This book will help you to discover how to stop and take action.

Chapter 1: Overthinking

Overthinking. It's the sleepless nights caused by past regrets that continue to haunt your mind. It's worrying about the potential future as you brood over negative experiences in the past. It's every paralyzing fear. It's always thinking that you'll fail no matter what, whether it be failing a class, at a job, or in relationships. There are often unrealistic expectations for success underlying overthinking, which must be met, and it takes an exhausting toll on you. It is both physically and emotionally exhausting because the brain that never slows or shuts down. Overthinking is the pause between texts as you wonder how they interpreted what you said. It's typing out and deleting a text, only to send another one because you are not comfortable with what you've written. It's the never-ending need for answers and responses to keep your mind satisfied.

Overthinking is the critical voice that brings you down because it doubts everybody and everything around you, especially yourself, bringing up your mistakes and decisions. When you overthink things, you never just go with your gut feeling. It's helplessly going down the self-destructive path your mind leads you down. It is like an uncontrolled wildfire that destroys all opposition in its path. Overthinking feels like you're always sitting tight for something, yet you don't really know what it is: for something to change, somebody to become distraught or a situation to end badly due to your own fault. Overthinking makes you feel unnecessarily sorry because you're upset for questioning and thinking the worst of people. It causes you to always imagine the worst-case scenario. Overthinking causes you to become excessively wary of everything. It's the dread of relationships since you require so much from a partner that you wonder if you would be better off alone. Because is it even possible to explain to a partner that it isn't you, I doubt or distrust, my mind is causing me to be so wary? How do you explain to a potential partner that you need to hear constant reassurance regarding your relationship or yourself? It's never certain whether someone truly likes you or is just tolerating you for the time being. As a result, you require consolation for each uncertainty. It always requires someone to be completely truthful and clarify any uncertainties about everything. Even if this might seem a bit too much, it is the only way to keep the painful assumptions caused by overthinking at bay. It believes situations that are genuine in your mind despite the fact that it's completely out there to a normal individual. Overthinking is caring too much about someone else's trivial opinion or an ignored text that shouldn't affect you, but in actuality, you are questioning what I have done wrong? And what can I do to fix it?

As you can see, overthinking is more than simply thinking too much about something, usually a negative experience such as past or current issues (ex. Finances, marriage, children, mistakes, regrets, etc.), events or conversations which grabs and holds your attention. Whether it be internally scolding themselves for a mistake they made yesterday or worrying over their performance tomorrow: an overthinker is characterized by these troubling thoughts—and their inability to stop thinking, which leaves them in a perpetual state of misery. Everybody overthinks from time to time, whether it be their decisions, present concerns, or behavior. This is predominantly true in this modern age, where the internet has resulted in information overload through social media and self-help information providing ample sources of anxiety and self-doubt. Modern life has also become overwhelmingly hectic and demanding with stressors arising from multiple sources: career, family, finances, mortgage, marriage, etc. Overthinking is quite literally an automatic habit that we have little conscious control of. Our brains are literally wired for overthinking with all our memories, thoughts, and emotions all interconnected into spiderweb networks of connections, which we refer back to in times of thought. However, although this ability made us more effective thinkers due to our ability to avoid painful outcomes (criticism, rejection, failure, illness, etc.) through our previous experiences, it can also paralyze our decision making.

Anxiety, worry, and self-doubt are feelings that are commonly experienced together by overthinkers as well and only exacerbates the problem. Anxiety is an emotion defined by an unpleasant and unrestful feeling, usually expressed as nervous behaviors such as physical distress, pacing back and forth, and deep reflection. It's a personal feeling of panic-stricken fear and apprehension at an expected future event, such as the feeling of your own impending demise. Anxiety and overthinking usually go together hand in hand. One of the most common signs of an anxiety disorder is a disposition towards overthinking. The brain that is constantly on-edge is hyperaware, continuously on guard for anything it seems to be unsafe or troubling. An overthinker would see issues even when there aren't any. Why? Because anxiety causes one to overthink everything in many different ways, and the result of this overthinking doesn't provide any closure or reassurance to your worries. Worry is strongly connected to anxiety and refers broadly to the continual and frantic images, feelings, and negative actions undergone by the mind to avoid or solve potential problems and their outcomes as part of an automatic risk analysis. For example, continually and frantically imagining your exam tomorrow and how you will act to succeed on it because you don't want to fail. However, there is always the looming feeling of actually failing or doing poorly on your exam, which results in feelings of distress and dread that grips you and won't let go while self-doubt is usually being unconfident or uncertain regarding one's own abilities, success, or actions. It is a pervasive feeling of failure and regret behind any new and bold pursuit you undertake because you feel like you aren't experienced or skilled enough to accomplish your goal. As you can see, the co-morbid conditions of overthinking: anxiety, worry, and self-doubt are all linked to the body's reaction to stress, which is a physical, mental, or emotional agent that responds to bodily or mental strain. It is the body's way of responding to any imminent threat or demand by switching into a rapid automated procedure best known as the "fight-or-flight response."

The fight-or-flight response is how the body protects you. It is intended to help you stay focused, energized, and aware in a potentially life-threatening situation to have the best survival chances. This can be through providing you additional strength to defend yourself, or driving you are to slam the breaks to avoid a car accident. Stress also gives you the capability to tackle obstacles. It's what keeps you motivated during exam studying time when you'd rather be slacking off, sharpens your concentration during an exam, and drives you to accomplish everything on your agenda. In this case, stress is a normal part of life that everyone experiences to give them the push to get through their day. But at some point, you can be under too much stress, and that's when it's no longer beneficial because it begins to cause major damage to your physical and mental health and well-being. In our modern lives, there are more causes of overwhelming stress than ever before, in the form of career expectations, children, finances, marriage, and relationships. This results in us being in a constant state of stress, which we can't unwind from because they are present everywhere, leaving us automatically overthinking in an attempt to find a solution or plan to solve our troubles amidst an ocean of anxiety, self-doubt, and possibilities. To a degree, this is a good thing because it allows us to reflect upon our problems and weigh potential solutions; in which case, overthinking is closer in nature to problem-solving or planning. We all require some degree of planning and thinking in our lives. However, the stressors of hectic and competitive modern life have given way to more reasons for sleepless nights spent excessively overthinking than ever before, with demands (e.g., career expectations, mortgage, finances, family, marriage, etc.) affecting every aspect of your life. This is especially true when it comes to taking decisive action, of which there are numerous potentially bad outcomes that anxiously immobilizes your decision-making. In this case, overthinking prevents us from taking decisive action when we need to rather than serving its original role in finding the best course of action. Social media and the internet only serve to exacerbate this problem by providing an over-idealized version of life and information overload in the form of self-help and improvement guides. The result is a perfect image or standard that we feel obligated to meet in order to fit in, but of which we always fall short of no matter what, resulting in endless anxiety, worry, and self-doubt.

While these are all key aspects of our lives that we all hope to be successful in, it is ultimately out of our control more times than not. We can't control our partners, bosses, children, markets, or economy, which determines the outcome of our lives. Regardless, they become the source of many of our sleepless nights spend overthinking and worrying as a result. It can start off as a random negative thought (Why did I make a mistake at work today?) which moves on towards anxiously obsessing over every small detail (circumstances, the order of events, emotional impact, what-ifs, effects, or consequences) of the experience in question rather than solving the actual underlying problem. At this point, it is key to point out that overthinking is often a symptom of a root mental problem such as depression, trauma, PTSD, agoraphobia, or an anxiety disorder characterized by constant and excessive stress, worrying, and dwelling on the past. There is also an element of self-doubt in overthinking as well due to over-analysis causing one to become unconfident of one's own capabilities and logic. Left unchecked, overthinking will cause you to become consumed by anguish, and unrealistic panic from everything that has gone or could go wrong, exacerbated by a mental problem. If you think rather than taking decisive action and accomplishing things, you are overthinking. If you analyze, reflect, and think about the same thoughts repeatedly rather than taking action, you are overthinking. This mental habit paralyzes you from taking action in your life. It also drains your energy, takes away your decision-making capability, and throws you into a never-ending loop of thinking the exact same thing. This cyclical thinking uses up all your time and energy and prevents you from making decisions, trying new things, and progressing in life. It's like a hamster running on its wheel, going around and round but remaining in the same place. As a result, overthinkers have an increased likelihood of worry, anxiety, and inner anguish compared to non-overthinkers.

Now that you know the processes, factors, and effects of overthinking, two dangerous thought patterns—ruminating and worrying eventually emerge in overthinking. Ruminating is carefully and obsessively going over a thought or problem repeatedly without ever finishing it. Whether it be repeating an old argument, comment, or mistake in your mind like a broken record, your mind just cannot seem to let it go no matter. Ruminating is heavily connected with depression due to the fact that the mental condition causes you to continually remember the worst aspects of yourself. Examples include:

I shouldn't have spoken up at yesterday's meeting. Everybody looked at me like I'm such an idiot.

I wish I had dropped out of university. I would've been so much further ahead in life by now if I had.

My parents said that I was worthless and couldn't amount to anything. I guess they were right.

You can see the self-defeating aspect of ruminating, one of the most dangerous aspects of overthinking because it paralyzes you from taking action. What's the point, if you'll just going to fail, no matter how hard you try or its already too late to turn around from a previous bad decision? As you can already tell, rumination is a reflection of how one views themselves and is thus deeply rooted in self-esteem and image. Negative self-esteem and image have several causes (media, belief systems, bullying), but the most common reason is your parents or guardians. Parents do have the largest impact on their children growing up after all. If they were abusive, neglectful, uninvolved towards you growing up, it'd result in lower self-esteem or image growing up. This is further possibly exacerbated if you have a history of academic, athletic, or social underperformance during your formative years and are compared to your higher-performing peers constantly. Without any obvious talents to make you think otherwise, it is easy to feel like you're a nobody in society compared to everyone else. As you already know, worry is your brain anticipating potential problems and outcomes in an effort to avoid them, but they tend to be negative - usually disastrous future predictions:

I'm going to fail the test tomorrow. I'll totally blank out, forget everything, and end up failing out of school.

I'll never get my driver's license. It is not important how hard I try or what I do. It's never going to happen.

I'll never get my dream job. There is always going to be someone better than me. I should just play it safe and work a stable and well-paying career I hate.

As you can see, ruminating and worry are closely related to each other; both cause one to think negatively, whatever it be about oneself or a situation. However, rumination and worry are only states of mind and can be resolved. This will be covered in a future cover. Ultimately, overthinking is defined by its two self-destructive patterns — worrying and ruminating, but it still serves an important role in problem-solving in our lives when engaged into an extent.

Chapter 2: Live Obligation

Many people mistakenly avoid adding a mindfulness practice to their daily lives because they think that mindfulness is some form of religious-based practice that can only be done if you are willing to devote to a specific faith. This could not be any further from the truth. The reality is that mindfulness is often associated with spirituality, but spirituality itself is not a religion. Furthermore, you do not have to have an active spiritual practice to benefit from mindfulness. On a very practical level, mindfulness is a series of tools and strategies that are used to ensure that you are engaging in the best life possible and that you are getting more from life. This is not necessarily a strictly spiritual practice, nor is it a strictly scientific practice. Instead, it is whatever you make it out to be. It can be as spiritual or practical as you desire for it to be.

Bringing practicality into mindfulness can be powerful in not only helping a more logical-oriented person take advantage of mindfulness but also in helping any person understand how mindfulness actually works. After all, there is a lot more behind the practices than just faith and belief. Mindfulness tools that are used in regular mindfulness practices have actually been proven to have very positive benefits on the health and wellness of individuals on many levels. Let's explore the many ways that mindfulness is truly a practical practice, and how you can begin using practical applications of mindfulness in your daily life.

How is Mindfulness Practical?

Despite a somewhat popular assumption that mindfulness is strictly a spiritual routine, mindfulness is actually incredibly practical. It is no secret that our society is buzzing with an enormous amount of stress. Anxiety, depression, and other mental illnesses are on the incline as people continue to be plagued by the many stresses of modern society. A lot of this can be attributed to a lack of mindfulness. With so many people living on autopilot, very few take the time to genuinely check in with themselves and get clear on what they need and what would make them feel happy. As a result, we have a tendency to chronically push away the things that we need most to maintain a happy and healthy life.

Mindfulness is the practice of bringing awareness back to your mind, body, and spirit, which means that you are intentionally checking in and looking for opportunities to de-stress and promote a happier and healthier life. Although it uses practices that are often associated with spirituality, such as meditation and positive affirmations, a lot of the practices are very practical in how they work in your mind. Essentially, you are intentionally slowing down and giving yourself the opportunity to bring peace into your life through mindfulness practices. The best way to do that is to quiet your mind using a variety of practices and techniques. Then, once you have mastered quieting your mind, you can begin asking yourself important questions like, "How am I, really?" "How do I feel about this?" or, "What is bugging me?" By bringing quietness to your mind first, the answers to these questions come a lot easier. Then, with the answers, you can begin enforcing change in your life that allows you to take peace out of the momentary practices of mindfulness and begin instilling it in other areas of your life, too. You begin to spread the peace around, and therefore increase the joy and happiness that you experience within your life.

Mindfulness is practical because it is a practice of truly caring for the health and wellness of your mind itself. Through a series of practices, you are training your mind to understand what peace is and to be able to tap into it any time that you feel it is needed.

What Are Some Practical Applications of Mindfulness?

Put simply, any practice that slows you down and encourages you to look within your mind and pay attention to yourself for a few minutes is a mindfulness practice. Some of these practices are more eccentric than others, and some are more practical. Since you are reading this guide, I am guessing that you are a person of logic and that you are looking for practical techniques that you can begin using so that you can tap into the realm of mindfulness right away.

Fortunately, there are many practical mindfulness techniques that you can begin using which will help you enjoy mindfulness on many levels in your life. These techniques take as little or as much time as you have to offer them, can easily be worked into any schedule, and are excellent for beginners or advanced mindfulness practitioners alike. The more you practice these techniques, the more value you will bring to your life from your mindfulness practice.

We are going to explore three mindfulness practices now that are highly valuable when it comes to integrating mindfulness into your life in a practical way. These include mindful breathing, mindful listening, and mindful appreciation.

Be in charge of your thoughts before you jump into the dark pit of overthinking, it is imperative for you to first clarify what you're actually overthinking about and also reflect on the negative ways overthinking is affecting your life. Such clarity will help enhance your determination to fight the tendency of overthinking.

Limiting Beliefs

The first thing you need to do is to pick out the "what if" questions you might likely ask yourself. Such questions are automatically stimulants of overthinking.

Ask yourself:

What are the common **"what if"** questions that I usually ask myself?

What circumstances or situations often **trigger** these questions?

It can be that you're overthinking because you often ask the wrong questions. Most often, rather than seeking solutions to the problem, you're busy painting "what if" scenarios in your mind, wondering about all the possible negative things that can occur.

So, take a deep breath and try to identify all the "what if" questions you often ask yourself. Also, try to detect specific circumstances that are likely to trigger such questions.

The next step is to dig into any limiting beliefs you might have, and try to gain a better understanding of some of the effect such thoughts have on your worries.

Ask yourself:

What are my "thoughts" about overthinking?

How do such beliefs affect the choices and decisions I make?

Do such thoughts have any advantages?

What are the long-term side effects of such beliefs?

When you are overthinking something, it is clear evidence that you're holding onto a certain set of beliefs which is affecting how you think and how you respond in such a situation. To face the fact, you're holding on to such beliefs because you feel they are of advantage to you. Probably, you feel they are advantageous because they give you a sense of control over certain circumstances or specific areas of your life (Based on the past). But sadly, such beliefs are hurting you because they hinder you from dealing with the major reasons why you're overthinking and that is a serious problem itself.

The best way to conquer your limiting beliefs is to challenge them head-on. Listed below are a few examples of certain questions you can ask yourself:

Why do I believe that I can't control overthinking?

Why do I believe that overthinking is beneficial?

Is there any evidence to back such thoughts?

Is the evidence credible and reliable?

Is it possible for me to view this situation from another angle?

Do I have any evidence that goes against my beliefs about this?

What do these tell me about my bad habit of overthinking?

All the thoughts that lead to overthinking are simply problems that you need to solve. But, if you're constantly swimming in a pool of uncontrollable worries, you will never be able to solve your problems.

Prepare to Train Your Brain To Establish A Healthy Relationship With Your Thoughts

Your thoughts are definitely different from reality. However, your thoughts can have a strong impact on you in real life, depending on how you view them.

Discard the saying that you're your thoughts. Rather, seek for ways to establish a connection with your thoughts and to maintain a healthy relationship with it.

If you observe that a particular thought keeps popping up in your mind, you can ask yourself these questions:

Do I perceive this thought as just a mental construct or I believe it to be the reality?

Do such thoughts keep me up all night, or do I just let them go?

Do I accept the thoughts just the way they come or attempt to change them?

Am I open to other thoughts or do I simply shut myself away from them?

What thoughts does this thought awaken in me?

After posing such questions, wait for the answers to come up— though the answers may not be obvious at first, posing such questions is very important. Gradually, you will be able to relate to your thoughts.

You can simply ask, "But is this true?"

The best kind of relationship you can establish with your thoughts is one that is full of acceptance and yet a measure of healthy distance. What this means is that you're open to any thoughts and you don't try to act as though they don't exist; however, you can also try as much as possible not to let them pull you down.

For instance, if you had a bad experience with a lousy cashier, you can begin to think that things might actually be better if only you had gone to another check-out, but you don't need to believe such mental interpretations because they are mere assumptions and not the ultimate reality. What are the possibilities? Probably this particular person is a wonderful cashier who is just having a bad day and maybe if you chose the other line you will still be on the queue. Such thoughts keep you open to possibilities.

When you compliment yourself or you acknowledge that you feel like you did well, you tend to enjoy such feelings.

For instance; when you tell yourself: "Well done me! I led the team and we achieved a major goal!" However, this doesn't mean your performance in the next game will be the same. It also doesn't make you a "better person" **because your self-worth is not attached to how well you can lead a team.**

Chapter 3: Symptoms Of Overthinking

Do you think that it is difficult to close off your mind at some random minute? Do you feel depleted and on edge as a result of your contemplations? Provided that this is true, you are likely unending over-thinker. Sadly, overthinking has turned into a worldwide plague, as we live in confusing occasions that require such a great amount of mental ability from us. Obligations, funds, passionate injury, and different issues leave our brains in a condition of overdrive. Through broad research, youthful and moderately aged grown-ups particularly play a part in overthinking. As anyone might expect, more ladies than men can be distinguished as over-thinkers.

The graph below shows the major symptoms of overthinking;

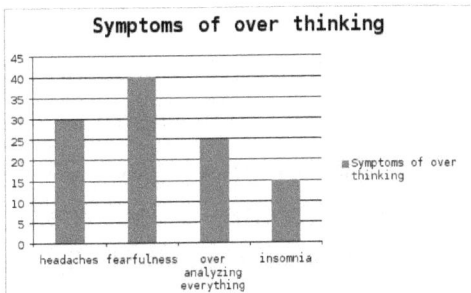

Symptoms of over thinking

Visiting headaches

If you are experiencing ordinary migraines, you likely think excessively. Migraines sign to our bodies that we need a break and this incorporates a rest from our own personalities. Additionally, on the off chance that you give close consideration to your musings, you likely consider very similar things and over.

Worriers will, in general, have negative idea designs that kept running in a circle, so as to battle this, attempt to fortify positive contemplations. Invest energy in your breathing and concentrating on care, and you should see the cerebral pains leave in a matter of moments.

Being fearful

In the event that you live in dread of things to come, at that point, you unquestionably are caught in your brain. Scientists found that this dread makes over-thinkers go-to medications or liquor so as to suffocate their negative considerations.

For this side effect of overthinking, you should start up a reflective practice, or something different that empowers care and living right now. Different recommendations permit a window for the overthinking. Apportion a couple of minutes out of each day to get out the majority of your stresses, regardless of whether through composition or conversing with somebody. Thusly, you can continue with your day and leave the stresses in the residue.

Muscles and joints stiffening up

In all honesty, overthinking can influence your entire body. When your physical body ends up influenced by something, it moves into your passionate body, and until the fundamental issue gets tended to, you will continue having a throbbing painfulness. Overthinking may begin in your cerebrum, yet its belongings creep into different pieces of your body, which leaves you feeling depleted and dormant.

Take a stab at extending each prior night bed, and getting customary exercise. This will advance a solid body, and consequently, a sound personality. The brain and bodywork in all respects firmly together; in the event that one is out of parity, the other will tumble to the wayside, as well.

Overanalyzing everything

Over-thinkers have one fundamental issue: they have a need to control everything. They need to plan out the future, but since they cannot anticipate it, this causes them extraordinary tension. They do not care for managing anything they cannot control. They have a noteworthy dread of the obscure, which makes them sit and think about every one of the alternatives as opposed to making a move. Truth be told, overthinking prompts poor basic leadership and decisions.

When you get yourself overthinking, attempt to take yourself back to the present minute through full breaths and thinking about something that loosens up you. Attempt to consider how these contemplations will serve you right now, and this by itself ought to dispose of them, as you will see that they do not do anything for you yet motivation incredible pressure.

Customary insomnia

Over-thinkers know the trouble of nodding off great. Sleep deprivation takes a hang on you since you cannot close off your cerebrum, and the contemplations gradually deaden you. Your mind races and you feel too tired to even consider sleeping; every one of the stresses from the day continues flooding your brain and you cannot escape from this psychological jail.

On the off chance that this sounds like you, take a stab at doing loosening up exercises before bed, for example, ruminating, yoga, shading, drawing, composing, perusing, or notwithstanding conversing with a friend or family member. Accomplish something that removes the move from your considerations and onto something different that enables your imagination and feelings to rise to the top.

Always second-guessing yourself

On account of their longing for flawlessness, over-thinkers continually break down, reanalyze, and triple investigate any circumstance. They would prefer not to settle on the off-base choice, so they set aside a long effort to settle on any decision since they do not confide in themselves. They are withdrawn from their instinct, so every choice originates from the mind, and this is not generally something to be thankful for. On the off chance that the mind is so foggy and hindered that you cannot settle on a reasonable choice, at that point you are certainly an over-thinker.

Figure out how to confide in your instinct, and go with your gut. In the event that notably, contrarily, in any event, you will have gained from the experience, and have more life exercises added to your repertoire.

Failure to stay in the present moment

In the event that you cannot remain right now and appreciate life as it comes, at that point you are a casualty of overthinking. Thinking an excessive amount of makes you lose the focal point of your general surroundings and become caught in your psyche. Getting to be stalled with considerations expels you from the now, and can upset your associations with others.

Make sure to open your psyche and heart to your general surroundings, and not get so enveloped with negative thinking. Just permit contemplations into your cerebrum that serve your prosperity, and attempt to disregard the ones that just cut you down. Life offers so much excellence and the open door for fantastic encounters, yet you can possibly welcome this in the event that you figure out how to block out of your mind and into your heart.

Likewise, associations with others help to quietness those negative musings. When we focus on others, we offer ourselves a reprieve and along these lines put the attention on another person. Figure out how to really tune in to other people, bond with them, and ask them inquiries about their lives. We can stop this endless overthinking issue together by shaping networks once more, and figuring out how to help and associate with each other.

Center around doing things that make you feel better and urge you to stay dynamic. Begin an activity program, join gatherings to interface with similarly invested individuals in your locale, eat well nourishments, have a care practice, and above all, figure out how to develop a positive association with yourself. Take a gander at your considerations as instruments to enable you to develop, not as adversaries that ruin your advancement.

Exhaustion

When we feel tired routinely, this requires an activity plan on our part. Our bodies need us to tune in and tune in to their sign, rather than continually going starting with one movement then onto the next and disregarding its calls. While weakness can likewise be brought about by working excessively and not resting, overthinking can likewise cause weariness. When you consider different things troubling you too frequently, you do not give your mind a rest. Your psyche cannot run all day; you will, in the long run, get worn out.

When we lived out in nature, we did not have such a great amount to stress over, and hence, we had less to consider. In the advanced world, we have confused lives that expect us to do as such much in so brief period, but since of this, we have significantly, even more, a need to back off and focus on our prosperity. On the off chance that you feel exhausted, back off and make sense of what your body and mind need from you.

Dread of failure

Over-thinkers likewise, have a perpetual want for flawlessness in all that they do. They cannot acknowledge disappointment, and make every effort to keep away from it. Incidentally, this typically includes sitting idle. Keep in mind, dread deadens the over-thinker, so as opposed to gambling disappointment, they'd preferably not set themselves in a place to bomb by any means.

In the event that this sounds like you, recollect that you are far beyond your mix-ups and disappointments. Additionally, remember that to go anyplace throughout everyday life, you need to commit a few errors. These enable you to develop, learn, and achieve new statures in your advancement.

Chapter 4: Practical Guide To Develop

Productive Habits

One of the many hard things for most of the people today is to change their already existing habits of a personal kind. Whether it involves the implementation of some new and good form of habit or it is just breaking away from the old and bad ones, it might feel like an impossible task for switching all your routines, which you actually followed for several years. But, it is not actually impossible to create or drop the habits; all that it takes is just a bit of willpower along with lots of dedication. We are actually what we do repeatedly. And, so does excellence, which not just an act but a solid habit. In our regular lives, it might be tough to build up new habits as there will be various forms of distractions that will lead all of us off from the narrow and straight path of achievement and will bring us back to the old path.

Wouldn't it be great if everything that we do could be automated? Starting from the way in which you start off your day to how you function the whole day and ending with the way in which you put a full stop to your day. For alleviating all the troubles which human beings generally face while changing their habits or developing productive habits, there are certain tips and tricks which you can actually follow for succeeding in this venture of yours. Let's have a look at them.

Intentional repetition of all the good habits at least for 30 times in a day

Human beings come with the characteristic of having any repetitive event for at least 30 times right before it turns out to be normal. For instance, an executive who keeps on speaking without any kind of variation in his voice is most likely to bore the audiences. If the executive really wants to get the posture and use up gestures for creating vocal variations, he/she needs to engage in that way in both formal and informal settings. The executive will be able to stick to that habit after he does the same for about 30 intentional forms of instances. When you want to develop something good, try to stick to that thing for at least 30 times a day, and you will find yourself in getting accustomed to the same.

Understanding the payoffs of associated nature

Each and every human behavior is being governed by the payoffs. Human beings stay pleasant to others as they receive a payoff. Human beings are also rude to others as we receive payoffs. So, in case you are trying hard to adopt a new habit or drop any existing one, try to dig in deep and understand the associated form of payoffs along with the habits. You can then easily decide to either connect with the receiving payoff or cut off yourself from the same.

Understanding your very own values

All our choices actually help in revealing all of your values along with our priorities. If you are trying to break off from a habit, all you need to do is to first understand what is actually important about the very habit of yours. Many a time, it will be comfort in which you might feel comfortable in keeping up with a particular habit. Try to replace the same with a priority, which is of much higher value for you.

Improving your environment

The fastest way for building good habits is to start by constructing consciously your existing environment, which includes your office, home, group of friends, transportation, and many others. All that you can do is to change your daily routine. When you let all those things go off, which actually holds you back, you will naturally look out for the new options which are available for nourishing your mind and body. For example, if you are a person who loves to watch videos all the time, you can change that habit by removing all the major sources of video from your life and shift to listening to podcasts. When your life isn't able to find the regular things with which it became habituated to, you will easily adapt to the new things for filling up the gap in your life.

Setting your intentions and scheduling all your habits on the calendar

Habits are most likely to develop by the repetition of the same kind of actions continuously. When you decide to cut off with a bad habit or start with a new one, you need to be intentional for achieving the results. For the purpose of stopping any bad form of habit, you need to set up the intention of changing it and also replacing the same with a new and good one. When you stick on to a regimented form of plan, you can easily form productive habits by simply scheduling any task on the calendar, which will also be reminding you of what you are supposed to do.

Setting up eventualities of if/then

The prime obstacle which comes in the way of forming or breaking any habit is the moment when you get tempted or when you slip up. So, it is always better to set up the possible form of scenarios from before only so that it becomes easier for you to take out the uncertainty out of your way. For instance, when you get tempted to eating a large piece of cake, just try to replace the scene by drinking a glass of water and then just count up to 10. When you are able to notice and break away from the impulse, there are high chances of you in reducing the breaking off of your word.

Having a powerful form of 'why'

When you fail in committing to a powerful form of why you will be doing something, suppose any habit which you want to throw away or build, it will be nearly impossible for you to stick to it. If you by yourself can manifest a powerful form of why and also commit to the very reason why you need to change or make a new habit, the probability of ending a habit or gaining a new one turns out to be more.

Making your very new habit the very first thing which you do every day

When looking forward to starting off a brand new habit for the first time in your life, the easiest way in which you can do so is to start off your day with the new habit every day. Your new habit, for example, exercising, praying, meditating, etc. needs to be the very first thing which you do every day as you get up. This will help in giving your brain the very importance of the new habit, and it can adapt to it in a faster way.

Pairing or replacing

Pairing or replacing can be regarded as two of the most effective ways in which you can replace a habit or build a new one. For instance, if you need to jog more and you just love to listen to podcasts, make a rule that you can only listen to your favorite podcasts when you jog. You can try out many other alternatives for the already existing habits or try to pair them with something which you love the most. This helps in developing a determination to practice the new habit.

Getting a partner who is accountable

When you try to adapt some productive habits all by yourself, you might not succeed all the time, or you might not be able to commit to that habit. You are most likely to get more motivated when you can find a person of supportive nature who can hold you accountable to all your goals. Try to explain and share your goals with that person. You can ask your partner to hold you accountable for your goal with the help of phone calls, email check-ins, a motivational form of conversations, and various other things. Motivation from a supporting person can help you in achieving your goals much faster than usual.

Starting off small and building good habits slowly

You can start by building up a keystone habit of good nature. The keystone form of habits comes with a rippling effect on the lives of individuals who are trying to start something new. In case your goal is to get healthier, you can start by drinking a glass of water every day when you wake up in the morning. As you become successful for a period of two weeks, you can up the game by adding another glass of water to your already existing habit of consuming one glass of water. The primary goal of this is to slowly reinforce your mind that keeping up with good habits is better for you and is easy as well.

Keeping up with the practice even when you fail

The productive form of habits arises right from the brain patterns which are grooved in and also takes up something for interrupting and creating the new neural form of pathways. It involves plenty of repetition, along with continuity. The main goal is to keep on practicing and also giving yourself the chance to fail. And, all that you are required to do is to just keep on practicing. The main difference between ending up a bad form of habit or starting off with a new good habit might be a gap of one practice only. So, don't just stop if you fail.

Try to give all your focus on the 3 Ps

When you are determined to change a habit of yours, just try to focus on the 3 Ps, which are practice, patience, and perseverance. Patience is needed as it takes up some time to build new habits. Practice is needed as it is needed to keep up the activity in a recurring order in order to shift your habit from being mindful of being habitual. Perseverance is required, as you are most likely to face lots of moments of frustration along with setbacks in your way. Try to keep up with all of these, and you can easily hold up the new habit.

Creating a list of wins

Wins are most likely to create momentum. For the very purpose of getting inspired to create productive habits or to break away from a bad habit, you are needed to focus on the daily number of wins. When you win for a day, your one win can help in changing your entire life. Each and every individual is required to know their list of wins, and also they would like to achieve the win. When you can develop the clarity regarding what you actually want to achieve, it will help in increasing all the odds of achieving the same.

Starting off from the present

You can start by assessing if you are ready or not to bring about the new habit. In case you are still thinking about the change, and you are also finding yourself in a defending position from the current form of patterns along with your systems of beliefs, you are not actually ready now. For the goal of creating a long-lasting change in your behavior, you are required to be committed first for changing yourself, and then only you can prepare your mind to take up the required actions for transforming the changes into a regular habit. Just start off from where you are at the moment and follow the path.

Swishing

You can visualize yourself in performing the bad form of habit. The very next moment, try to visualize your very own self where you are actually trying to push away the bad habit and also performing the alternative. You can end the sequence with the very picture of yourself where you are in a state of high positivity. You can run this exercise several times in a day, and you will notice that your tendency to practicing bad habits is going away slowly with time. Picturizing yourself gives you an image of your future, which will guide your brain in stopping from performing the bad habit for your very own good.

Doing it for yourself

Stop worrying about all such things which you think should have as your habits. Try to tool all your habits right towards your very goal along with all the things which actually motivate you. Empty kind of resolutions is not at all enough in sticking the productive habits with your life. You need to realize that it is for your very own good. You are the one who is responsible for breaking yourself down and also building yourself up.

Knowing all the benefits

Try to get yourself accustomed to all the benefits which you can achieve from changing a habit of yours. When you are able to figure out the benefits, you can easily notice a change in your energy levels along with your enthusiasm for adapting to the change.

Write them down

Many people tend to achieve what they want in life by simply writing their goal on a piece of paper and keeping the writing in front of them. It actually helps your mind to adapt to your enthusiasm for getting the change and also helps in increasing your motivation.

Processing the plan

The step which most people skip while fantasizing about having a productive form of habit is that they do not answer clearly why they actually want this change in their lives. It might look like a very small detail, but in reality, it actually plays a deep part in keeping up with your motivation over the course of time. Only visualizing what you want to achieve is not going to help. Try to plan out the image along with the end results properly.

Running the change as a new form of experiment

It might happen that you want to bring about a change in your habits, but you are not sure about the end results. You can overcome this by adapting the new change as an experiment, which you can carry on for a week or two. You can easily assess the results, which will be in the form of changes in your life and try to compare the same with your past. Is it better than before, or it is of no use in your life? When you run a new habit as an experiment, you can get a clear idea about the results and can also gain the required motivation by getting sure about the end results in the long run.

Using 'but.'

The best way in which you can bring about a new change in your life is by thinking about your current condition with 'but.'

For instance, you can use but for interrupting all your negative thoughts like, 'I am not at all good at doing this, but if I keep on working, I might succeed one day.' This actually works like magic as it helps in contrasting your present situation with the future where you can easily see the end result and get motivated in going with the change.

The habits that you adopt for yourself are for your own good. If you think of any of your habits as ruining your life, do not think twice and just start working on from now only. If you start now, you can easily enjoy the majority of your life under the lights of positivity with no shadows of negativity around you.

Chapter 5: How Overthinking And

Worrying Are Holding You Back

About everyone that has ever existed worried about a variety of things at some point in their lives,. There is no immunity to it whatsoever, so don't feel you are in it alone. Worrying and overthinking, like alcohol, harm you slowly but surely. They come gently and then turn into a habit and before you know it, you don't even know you've got it.

However, what makes some people less of an addict than others is that while some have control over the bottle, others are puppeted by it. You have to learn to take charge of your thoughts, because only then can you define how they affect you. To understand how overthinking holds you back, you have to know the signs and symptoms which indicate that it is actually a problem. Knowing the symptoms can also help you monitor yourself, so you don't go overboard and lose yourself in the process. Take a look at the symptoms outlined below:

1. Sleeping disorders or an inability to sleep:

If you overthink or worry to the point where your mind becomes an inhibition to sleep, then that is a flare signal to take seriously. Being unable to turn off your mind and have good sleep doesn't bode well for anyone. And if you also have a disordered sleeping style in which your sleep is often punctuated by worries, it is a sign that you overthink and worry too much.

2. Engaging is self-medication:

Research carried out on causes of overthinking disorders is of the opinion that people will often turn to food, alcohol, drugs, and other external means of managing their emotions, the reason being that they are unable to calm themselves using their internal resources.

3. Extreme tiredness:

If you are almost always tired, it may be proof of your insomnia or the aftereffects of going round and round that circle of vague thoughts.

4. Perfectionism and the urge to control everything:

You will often find that you want to plan every detail of your life as it is the only thing that gives you a sense of calmness. However, it doesn't quite work because perfection cannot be achieved, and it is impossible to take control of everything.

5. You are obsessed with thoughts of failure:

As you try to explore your way towards being perfect, you will often be obsessed with negative thoughts of failure. Your fear of failure and the unknown will tend to paralyze and inhibit you from learning from your past or moving on from your failures.

6. Fear of the future:

Your fear of the unknown tends to materialize as the fear of the future.

Rather than be excited about the potential the future holds, you will tend to be caught in your own anxieties about all the things that could go wrong.

7. Self-doubt and lack of self-trust:

With overthinking comes the problem of doubting yourself and your own judgments. You spend your time second-guessing everything down to even the most trivial things. You are worried about everything and anything and depend on the validation and reassurance of others to accept your own judgments.

8. Tension headaches are a norm:

If you often feel like there is a tight band placed around your temples and a slight pain and stiffness often strike your neck, chances are high that you overthink. The tension headaches are signs that you need to cut back and relax. The sky isn't going to cave in.

Having considered the symptoms of overthinking and worrying, let's see how they both hold you back.

1. They inhibit you from experiencing new things:

Do you ever find yourself turning down a great and fun activity because you overthought and came up with a million other reasons why it's best you don't attend? It is like turning down a visit to the beach because according to stats, the beach kills lots of people every year. Want to know a fact? People die every year from different things, beach or no beach. So, that is just classical overthinking in play there. You get to keep your facts and be correct all right, but you missed a new experience and all the potentials it holds.

2. You miss out on learning new stuff:

To learn new things, you have to be willing to try new experiences. However, if you let your overthinking hold you back as was discussed above, you will find that you are passing on many different opportunities to learn great stuff. To learn, you will have to exit your shell and put aside your fears.

3. You experience a decrease in productivity:

You may not realize it, but overthinking can be a great time killer. Rather than investing your efforts and ideas into a productive cause of action, you will spend too much time pondering on the possible outcomes, the potential of failures, and the viability of your ideas. Don't confuse overthinking for careful planning; they are distinct. Take your time and make your plans carefully, but don't spend all your time pondering and taking no actions. Get stuff done.

4. It induces self-doubt:

Have you ever been at such a point of indecisiveness that it annoys everyone around you? That is overthinking at work right there. You had a number of choices, say, ice cream or chips for dessert, but you just couldn't make up your mind. The waiter looks patient, but you can tell they find you infuriating. Your date doesn't exactly look like they are enjoying themselves either, all because you could not make up your mind in time. Your self-doubt transcends beyond the mere action of making a choice of dessert, though. It is somewhat similar to how you would imagine yourself failing when you are ill prepared for a test or how demoralized you are about trying again when a college rejects your admission. When your thoughts become infused with fear, you will find that you have limited how far you can go. Your fears will become inhibitive factors which could cause you to pass up on opportunities because you fail to see the bright side or are just too afraid to try. You end up being a swirl of negative energy, all born from worrying and overthinking.

5. You stress yourself out:

Overthinking is an indication that you have a gazillion and one vague and unnecessary thoughts running around haphazardly in your head. This spells one thing for you — stress. We sometimes get so caught up thinking too much that we miss enjoying the beautiful moments because our minds are so clogged up we don't sense them.

Chapter 6: Identify And Change Your

Beliefs And Negative Thought Patterns

It is one thing to identify a negative thought pattern and it is another to change a belief or negative thought pattern. In this chapter, we will look at how to identify and change your beliefs and negative thought patterns.

Research consistently links negative thinking to increased risk of mental health problems, physical health issues, relationship problems, and financial trouble, but like every other problem, there is always a solution. Cognitive-behavioral therapist Amy Morin created the acronym BLUE, which stands for: Blaming myself, Looking for bad news, Unhappy guessing, and Exaggeratedly negative.

•**Blaming myself:** We can agree that it is important to take responsibility for our actions, but then going to extremes with it isn't a good thing, it can lead to mental health problems such as depression. Be alert because we often blame ourselves without realizing it, even in situations where there is little or nothing you could have done. Examples include times when you say things to yourself like "You have ruined it all", "You can never do anything right", etc.

•**Looking for bad news:** Often, we tend to focus on the bad things and leave out the good ones, even in situations where the good overshadows the bad. Living with this mentality will leave you stuck with negative thoughts. Most times, it is required that we step back and form a more balanced and more realistic outlook towards things or situations.

•**Unhappy guessing:** The future is unknown to us, but we can always predict what we think it is going to look like. Most times, we find ourselves in situations where we predict something negative, like how you might have gotten bad grades in your exams, or how you will not get that promotion or salary increase you have been yearning for. The truth is, unhappy guessing can become a self-fulfilling prophecy if you're not careful.

•**Exaggeratedly negative:** The kind of things you say to yourself count, like telling yourself that everything about your present relationship is not working, or the examination you wrote was terrible. Things like this lead to a downward spiral and such negative thoughts don't make you better, they tend to make you feel worse and the more you keep feeling this way, the less likely you are to take positive action.

Beliefs have a more negative impact on your life than any other factor that you can think of. We live every day with a large number of beliefs that limit our ability or potential. They come from a lot of sources as well as from our interpretation of the world around us. Humans were created in such a way that we can't help but constantly learn new things, but sometimes we learn things that are inaccurate and unsuitable for our lives. Well, the good news is that you can completely remove limiting beliefs and replace them with beliefs that make you a better version of yourself.

To change something, the first step is to identify it and be able to detect what a negative thought or belief is. Then, you can go further in changing it. It's always advisable to try and maintain relevant thoughts as there are over a million limiting beliefs that we tend to worry about but are irrelevant. We should only worry about beliefs or thoughts that will have an impact, and a good one at that. The moment you are able to deal with this aspect, there wouldn't be an issue in dealing with others.

If there is an aspect of your life that you are not happy with and you are not making an effort to do something about it, then it's appropriate to say that you have limiting beliefs; otherwise, it makes sense that you would do something to change the situation.

A major indicator of negative thoughts and beliefs is your behavior; consider how you're doing in different areas of your life such as finances, relationships, health, fun, and adventure. Are you feeling financial pressure in your life? Have you been able to meet up with that savings target that you set for yourself? In your relationships, consider your romantic relationship and also relationships with family and friends, are they satisfying you? Or maybe it is in the aspect of health - do you have that perfect summer body you want? Is your weight bothering you? Or are you missing the fun in your life; are you not doing the things you want to do? Is it that dream trip to the Bahamas you've been dreaming of that is out of reach or that musical instrument that you have learned to play but haven't been able to own? And it might not be any of these things but another part of your life that you're not satisfied with. If there is something that is bothering you, then limiting beliefs and negative thoughts could be behind it.

Negative thoughts are usually associated with negative consequences, they are oftentimes based on false beliefs or even selective facts, and they don't give room for important facts that can lead to better consequences. When you begin to think rigidly, there is a tendency to take an all-or-nothing approach and you are not going to make room for change. We often see this in different aspects of our lives, a good example is in failed relationships, you come up with conclusions like you are not good at relationships, you are probably not good at being a good partner, or feel you cannot be loved. With these thoughts running through your head, there will never be room for you to focus on being better or taking advice from others.

For a lot of people, it is very difficult to recognize negative thoughts; you tend to just see that things aren't working well in your life. Cognitive therapy is designed to help you recognize these negative thoughts and help you develop a healthier pattern of thinking.

There are common types of negative thinking, all alike but with borderline differences among them, and sometimes a thought can involve more than one type of negativity.

Four Common Negative Thinking Patterns

1. **All-or-Nothing Thinking:** This involves you trying to be perfect in all you do, forgetting that if perfection existed for everyone, then by definition, perfection wouldn't exist. You have it in your head that, "I have to do things perfectly, and anything less is a failure."

2. **Focusing on the Negatives:** You accumulate disappointments and believe that nothing goes your way. It feels like one disappointment after another.

3. **Negative Self-Labeling:** You have resulted in viewing yourself in a negative

light. You end up saying, "I'm a failure. If people knew the real me, they wouldn't like me. I am flawed." Even when people get to know the real you, you will have doubts about who you really are because you don't think highly of yourself.

4. **Catastrophizing:** This is when you only expect the worst to happen – "If something is going to happen, it'll probably be the worst-case scenario." There is no positivity in this form of thinking.

There are other negative thinking patterns that CBT experts have discovered, such as excessive need for approval, mind reading, should statements ("People should be fair, and when they are not fair they should be punished."), disqualifying the present, dwelling on the past, and pessimism ("Life is a struggle. I don't think we are meant to be happy. I don't trust happy people. If something good happens in my life, I usually have to pay for it with something bad.").

Changing Beliefs and Negative Thoughts

When there is a problem, there are means of creating a solution. The most basic way to bring about change is to begin replacing the negative thoughts with more positive thoughts. When we say positive, we also mean realistic, like when you come up with thoughts like, "I can't save enough for that dream trip", you might want to respond by telling yourself, "I can devise a plan to save money for my trip". This is the key to creating the kind of life you will enjoy and want to live.

A lot of people have come up with different ways to get rid of these negative thoughts or beliefs, such as methods that include: distractions, diversions, or drowning in their sorrows and getting stuck in their negativity. These activities only reduce the pain and numb yourself temporarily, and while you think the pain or thoughts are not there, it lingers and returns to you stronger than before and even worse, could remain there for the long-term.

In changing a negative thought or belief, the first step is usually to identify what these thoughts are. They are usually repetitive and unhelpful; hence, they bring about unpleasant emotions like anxiety, depression, shame, fear, anger, unworthiness and so on. The moment we learn to identify and stop these negative thought patterns as they begin to occur, we can take a step back from them. This process of stepping back from thoughts is called 'cognitive defusion' – a process that helps you realize that the thoughts in your head are nothing more than just thoughts. They are not real and are not in any way close to reality. Note that it is normal to have negative thoughts, it is part of you as a human, thus the problem is not that you are having negative thoughts; the problem arises when you start believing in those thoughts and see them as the truth. Anxious thoughts and worries also have to be put away. Worry is a situation when the mind projects into an imagined future and makes up scenes or scenarios about things that could go wrong. That's when 'what if' thoughts come up. You tend to think things won't work out in your favor or nothing good will come out of whatever situation you're in. In the end, nothing might happen, but you are still stuck with the thoughts you have conjured in your head.

Another step to changing your negative thoughts or beliefs is coming to your senses. A lot of negative thoughts flow in two directions, it's either that you're dwelling on the past, probably on a mistake you made, a problem you had, or something wrong that went on that is taking a toll on you; or you're worried about the future, thinking of things that could be and the ones that will not, what will happen if... and more. This is definitely going to stress you out and while this is going on, you lose focus on the present, which is where your attention should actually be, because, in days, weeks, months, or even years from now, you will also have to come back to think of this present day that you're not bothered about right now and your cycle of worry and stress will continue repeating.

The goal here is to step out of these negative thoughts by coming to your senses, redirect your attention out of the thoughts in your head, focus on the present and make it count. Be aware of things around you; be fully in the moment, this is also a form of mindfulness practice.

Regular mindfulness practice is another key step to changing these negative thoughts, as we live and grow up, we get more and more drawn into things that happen in our lives, our problems, goals, hopes, fears, and even desires which could mean a lot when we take them very seriously, hence, losing touch with a deeper sense of self. This way, it becomes very easy for you to get dragged into your negative thoughts and lose yourself when it comes to the mind. Research from Harvard University shows that most people are 'mind wandering' about 47% of their day and this is the root of what causes cognitive fusion (entanglement with thoughts). Mindfulness practice involves waking up to a feeling of wholeness and peace, involving waking up from that mind-wandering state, a state that contains our false beliefs, habits, reactions, and even negative thinking patterns. Regular mindfulness practice will help you build your capacity to live in that deeper awareness and tame the mind.

Finally, there are some thinking patterns that can be very persistent, and even if you have tried to control it feels like there is no way around it. There are certain questions that you can use to question these negative thoughts and deter your focus from them. Some of them include:

- Is this true? (Can I know that it's true?)

●Is this thought in any way useful or helpful?

●Is this just an old event that my mind is playing out of habit?

●Does this thought help me take effective action?

Asking these questions below can also help to create a new thought pattern of possibilities. They will help focus on more positive, logical, and constructive thoughts and help you effectively face your daily challenges and live a meaningful life. Remember that it is all about choosing which one will work for you depending on the situation.

●What is the actual truth?

●What exactly am I trying to achieve in this situation? How do I go about achieving that?

●How can I make the best of this situation?

●Who would I be without these negative thoughts?

●How can I see this in a different or new way?

●What are the things I'm grateful for in this moment?

When these questions are asked and answered, there is a big change and you tend to focus and move easily away from the negativity and now strive towards a positive light.

Chapter 7: Neuro-Linguistic Programming

What is Neuro-Linguistic Programming (NLP)?

Neuro-Linguistic Programming is a relatively new science that studies the brain and how it reacts and works in certain situations. It was founded first in the seventies and has since been popularized by people such as Tony Robbins, who uses his deep understanding of NLP among other techniques to help people move from a state of suffering to one of freedom.

If we break down each work, we can get a better understanding of what NLP is about.

Neuro stands for the connections in the brain. Our brain has billions of neurons that are each connected to one another in different sequences and paths. Our neuron connections are constantly changing and being updated based on the knowledge and experiences we acquire through our lives. For example, if I were to say the name Bill Clinton, you will likely have an associated neuron linking that name to a picture of what Bill Clinton looks like. You may also have other connections that are linked to his names such as his wife Hilary, his presidency or his marital affair. This shows how our brain works and how each thought can be connected to a whole host of other thoughts and memories.

Linguistic represents language. NLP is focused on learning the language of these brain neurons in order to better understand where people's negative thought processes come from and how to help them actively create new brain connections. The language of the brain is very difficult to understand because our brains are so complex and the language can offer differ from one person to the next. However, there tend to be some core patterns of how we think as humans that can be applied to all people. How we connect things such as public speaking to feelings of stress and anxiety to how we deal with a break up by feeling hurt and sometimes unworthy of love. Many of these feelings are part of the generic human condition and as such we can identify when they are occurring in others and why they are occurring. The more language patterns we find the more we can help others to break the pattern and recode new and more empowering patterns.

Programming is usually used in the IT world and refers to changing or updating old programs for computer software. However, seeing as NLP looks at the brain from a science perspective, we can view it as something similar to a computer. With certain processes and thoughts creating certain outcomes, we can therefore theoretically recode or program the brain to think different thoughts to create other, more desired outcomes. While NLP can sometimes be more of an art than a science, the programming of people's brains is often up to the person themselves. The role of NLP practitioners is not to act as a savior who will reprogram a person's brain to rid them of any negative or defeating thought patterns, rather it is their job to help empower people to learn and identify these patterns in themselves so that they can transform their own thoughts and thus their life experiences as a result.

NLP Presuppositions

NLP does not assume that everything it teaches is based on core, undeniable truths. It acknowledges the fact that many of its teachings can be subjective and because it is a science that is still evolving and changing it bases itself on many presuppositions. These presuppositions or beliefs of NLP are there to help empower individuals. Whether they are 100 percent true or not is irrelevant if the desired results can be obtained through the belief that they are true. While there are many NLP presuppositions, they can be categorized into six main ones. These are:

The map is not the territory

Taking on this belief tends to lead to a person become much more tolerant of other people and their different points of view. While many people believe that their point of view is correct and that it is the one true belief, this is almost always not true. Everyone experiences life through a different lens, as nobody has the exact same experiences. Even if they did, two people would interpret those experiences differently. Therefore, nobody can definitively say that their view of the world is how it really is. We are all only looking at a specific snapshot of the map and we cannot see the whole territory. We may say some of the main roads and towns but the Mao doesn't show us all the undulations of the hills and the potholes that exist along each road. Realizing that your view of the world is not exactly correct is the first step to opening your mind up to considering other people's opinions. All conflict is as a result of people believing their maps are the territory. Once we ditch this belief it allows us the freedom to grow and learn about other maps and other views of the world.

The past doesn't equal the future

Many people carry a false belief that what happened to them in the past is destined to happen to them again in the future. They believe that they are destined to repeat the same mistakes they have in the past because it's part of who they are.

They believe that their character and abilities are fixed. NLP goes against this belief and suggests that our past does not have to be a predictor of our future unless we want it to be. NLP believes that we can put in the effort to work on our past failures or mistakes so that we can prevent them from happening again. It believes in a person's ability to change negative thought patterns and extol limiting beliefs in order to be successful in the future. This belief is at the core of personal growth and an empowered mindset. Many people like to live with the belief that their past will equal their future because it takes the responsibility out of their hands. Realizing you can grow and develop any skill you need, requires you put in the work to get there. It is much easier to play the victim role and blame other people or external circumstances for your situation. For example, someone may say they will never get a good job because they always get too nervous in job interviews. This may be true for now but getting nervous in a job interview is something that many people experience and it is only by working on controlling the nerves that the desired future result can be met. Living with the belief that all job interviews in the future will go badly will ensure that is exactly what happens.

Everything is Achievable

NLP practitioners believe that anything and everything is achievable. Everything in life is simply a problem to be solved. We might not know exactly how to achieve something right now but we know there are certain steps we can take to tackle the problem. Holding this belief allows people to open up their minds to unlimited possibilities for their futures. It helps people realize that there is no limit to their potential for personal growth and that any fears or worries they may be living with can be eradicated and pushed past. They can achieve anything they really put their minds to and they can grow into the amazing person they wish to become.

Empowerment comes from Responsibility
The role of an NLP practitioner is to help empower people to help themselves. While psychologists and some other professions try to solve people's problems for them, NLP practitioners try to get people to challenge their own existing mindsets and take responsibility for changing them. Rewiring your brain is not a quick fix solution. It as a process that you must live by daily and in order to achieve any form of long-term results, you must take responsibility for your mindset into your own hands. In Spiderman, there is a

great quote saying, "With great power, comes great responsibility." But in fact, the opposite is also true. With great responsibility, comes great power. By taking full responsibility for everything in your life you have the power to change it. This requires you to turn away from the victim mentality where you believe life happens to you. Empowered people believe life happens for them.

Age is not necessarily a good judge of maturity. We develop maturity as we accept more and more responsibility for our lives. While everything that happens to you in your life may not be your fault, it is still your responsibility to deal with what happens to you. To use an extreme example, you may become paralyzed in a car accident that was the result of a drunk driver crashing into you. You could live the rest of your life wallowing in self-pity and blaming the other driver for your situation and not too many people would blame you. But you can also decide to take responsibility for your new situation and decide that you are going to be happy despite your circumstances. You can decide you are going to figure out a way to walk again. You can find fun activities to do in the meantime to keep your spirits up. You don't have to be the victim of your circumstances.

People respond to perception, not reality

We tend to often judge what happens to us based on our perception of events. We judge other people based on what they say and do yet we judge ourselves based on our intentions. We hold ourselves to a different standard than we do others. For example, presume you were playing baseball with some friends. It's your turn to bat and you swing and miss the first ball. Someone behind you starts laughing. You immediately become angry and spiteful towards this person for laughing at your missed swing. In reality, the person was actually chatting with another friend and laughing at a story he was being told.

You never considered this possibility however and you judged his actions based on your own perception of reality. A perception that puts you at the focus. You may often think that everything people say or do is in a reaction towards you in some way. When the roles are reversed however and you are the one laughing just after a person swings, you won't see it as being rude because you were not intentionally laughing at them. You judge yourself by your intentions even when your actions may be rude towards the other person. NLP practitioners are aware that we respond to things based on our limited view of them and often from a directly personal perspective.

Chapter 8: Why Addiction Increases Your Anxiety

4.1 Types of Addictions

In the journey towards anxiety recovery, there are different kinds of treatment administered to a patient. Some of these treatments are drug-related. Therapists and doctors usually give patients medication such as Zoloft, Tofranil, Valium, and Xanax to help lessen symptoms of anxiety or panic disorders.

Although patients with anxiety disorders do not necessarily develop substance disorders, research has shown that there is a strong possibility between the two. An estimated 18 percent of Americans have developed substance use disorders because of anxiety or they end up getting anxiety because of substance use disorder. When this happens, it can be profoundly hard for doctors and health care providers to diagnose the cause of anxiety in their patients when there is a substance use disorder all because it is hard to tell the difference between symptoms of intoxication and the symptoms of anxiety.

When it comes to anxiety, there are several types such as generalized anxiety disorder, post-traumatic stress disorder as well as obsessive-compulsive disorder. Different people with different types of disorders experience anxiety in various forms. One thing in common is that they all feel worried and fear without the visibility of clear danger.

People who have a physical or mental illness also have a tendency of suffering from anxiety and this makes the diagnosis as well as a treatment even more difficult. There could be other problems that need to be treated first before treatment for anxiety can begin. Substance abuse then adds another complicated variable to the treatment equation. People who have anxiety and also have some form of substance use disorder should seek immediate and professional treatment. So what are the types of addiction? It is hard to pinpoint addiction based on anxiety or caused by anxiety. However, the most well-known addiction that many people go through is related to alcohol as well as drugs. The most common drug addictions are:

nicotine, found in tobacco

THC, found in marijuana

opioid (narcotics), or pain relievers

cocaine

4.2 How Addiction is Created in the Brain

When a person is addicted to substances and behaviors, it creates a pleasurable yet short 'high' that is both psychological as well as physical. If you have an anxiety disorder, there is typically more use of certain drugs administered to you that you get high on more frequently to achieve that sense of high or to achieve a sense of relief from your symptoms. Over time, the addiction becomes difficult to stop.

The Brain

Some people who take on anxiety medication never approach it again while others tend to be addicted to it because the need to lead a more normal life is obsessive and they procure these medications in various, often illegal ways. This addiction is partially due to the brain's frontal lobes which allows a person to delay or lessen the symptoms of reward or gratification. When there is an addiction, the frontal lobe malfunctions and gratification is achieved immediately.

Apart from the frontal lobe, there are other areas of the brain that play a role in addiction. The nucleus acumens as well as the anterior cingulate cortex which causes pleasurable sensations is responsible for increasing a person's response when they are exposed to addictive substances.

Chemical imbalances in the brain, as well as mental disorders such as bipolar and schizophrenia, are also other possible causes of addiction. These disorders can bring about coping strategies that are highly dependent on addiction.

Addiction Is the Result of Neuroplasticity

Neuroplasticity is the ability of your brain to change its physical structure and function based on life experiences, thoughts, emotions as well as repetitive behaviors. What we do on a daily basis whether good or bad gets wired into our system and the structure of our brain because of this neuroplasticity ability. Neuroplasticity is the foundation of all learning and it also creates an amazingly resilient brain. It creates the ability for people to recover from traumatic experiences such as injuries as well as birth abnormalities. It also gives humans the ability to improve neurological deficits and reverse behavioral patterns. The very same elements that make the brain strong are the same characteristics that make it vulnerable as well which is why researchers pinpoint neuroplasticity as the cause of addictions becoming ingrained in our brain as well as the reason why our brain loses valuable skills as we age and also the reason why we get some brain illnesses.

The time when the Brain's Reward System goes awry

Our brain is a highly skilled reward detector. A brain that is addicted has learned to prioritize and seek reward ahead of anything else. The brain also has a pretty primitive reward system that operates on a subconscious level and it operates on a subconscious level that was originally meant to push humans to seek out opportunities to extend their survival capacity. In today's world, however, we are all overwhelmed with many opportunities to survive from shopping to junk food, sex, drugs, and electronic gadgets.

Our addiction and cravings depend on an intricate interplay of the chemicals in our brain but dopamine, the feel-good neurotransmitter is at the center of all of them. Dopamine is considered a chemical messenger that transports signals across synapses and it is the chemical that pushes forth reward-seeking and motivating behavior. Dopamine also affects the processes that govern movement and plays an extremely important role in Parkinson's disease. Dopamine also plays a crucial role in addiction as it heightens salience, which is the pull of a stimulus. When you attempt something pleasurable the first time, dopamine rewards come in after the event or activity. At subsequent experiences, dopamines are released much earlier until seeing a trigger or even just thinking about it causes the anticipatory dopamine surge.

4.3Rewiring Your Brain to Overcome Addiction

Addiction Treatments

Recovery from any kind of addiction does need extreme changes in feelings, thoughts as well as behaviors. You can adopt new behavioral patterns and thoughts as well as recruit neutral networks that encourage new connections as well as communication pathways that can change the brain's thinking prowess over time. Not one treatment works for everyone- each individual requires either two or more treatments and when it comes to addiction treatments, treatments focused on encouraging neuroplasticity have been proven to be successful.

Contemplative Practices

According to the American Journal of Psychiatry, studies have shown the connection between mindfulness and meditation with successful rehabilitation of addiction. Constant practice of meditation and mindfulness can alter the brain. With this in mind, practicing mental health tools that teach an individual to put time and distance between their impulses and themselves is extremely beneficial. This pause between action and urge encourage neuroplasticity as well as new behaviors. There is also a more prevalent kind of meditation that helps in overcoming addiction and this is called urge surfing.

Cognitive Behavioural Therapy

The theory behind CBT is to think about the situations that could affect the way we behave and the way we feel. When we are faced with an adverse situation, it is natural to experience negative emotions, and these feelings may lead to negative behavioral reactions. CBT looks at the way an individual distinguishes a scenario and how this perception has more to do with their personal reactions rather than the extent of the scenario itself.CBT aims to help people change or alter their own destructive thinking and behavior that would hopefully lead to an improvement in their mood and daily functioning. CBT involves plenty of problems -solving and it borrows many psychotherapeutic techniques from acceptance and commitment therapy and dialectical behavior therapy, compassion-focused therapy, Gestalt therapy, mindfulness and motivational interviewing.

TMS Therapy

TMS is called **Transcranial Magnetic Stimulation** (TMS) and it is an FDA approved therapy specifically for treatment-resistant depression and it has shown good results for treating addiction. This stimulation is non-invasive and an outpatient procedure where the cells of the brain are stimulated with magnetic pulses and it is given via electromagnetic coil. During a TMS session fluctuating magnetic fields are projective via the skull into a patient's prefrontal cortex. Don't worry, this is not a scary procedure as mentioned before, it is non-invasive. The magnetic fields that are projected will stimulate the cells in the brain and it helps to alter neuronal activity as well as blood flow.

Chapter 9: Fear And The Gang

Anxiety, fear, depression and anger—these emotions seem to be different, yet all of them seem to stem from the same place of uneasiness deep inside. These emotions are powerful and can become debilitating. When we first try to shake off the unpleasant or disturbing feelings but without success, don't we have a tendency to clam up, scared? I've been there, thinking I was losing my mind and afraid I will never be "normal" again. I was unable to control it, which made it even more frightening. I tried and tried to shake it off, but to no avail. Our bodies react to stress in various amazing ways and it's totally fascinating!

In my case, depression and anxiety were sort of playing a tug of war and anxiety usually won. Depression was lurking close by, ready to devour what was left of me after anxiety temporarily loosened its grip. I needed a break from these excruciating moods. I resolved to take action, even if it was the last thing my body wanted to do. I would put a grin on my face, resembling that of an orangutan taking a "selfie". But somehow the grin was working. A study at one of the universities revealed that clinically depressed patients who were required to stand in front of a mirror and grin from ear to ear felt significant improvement as compared to the other group of patients who were treated in the conventional way with medication. No wonder there is a saying "laughter is the best medicine."

Depression

To dread getting out of bed on a rainy morning is one thing, but when it lasts for days, without the energy to move, is another story altogether. It's a mystery that an overall healthy body can react this way. The motions of morning rituals took huge effort. Sometimes I'd be still wearing a robe, pajamas and slippers when taking my child to school, hoping not to be pulled over...

When the last thing on my mind was to do something, that is exactly when something had to be done! I had to resolve to roll out of bed regardless how low I felt. This perpetual numbness had to end somehow, preferably sooner. It required action. I resolved to take action even if it was the opposite of what my body wanted to do. I forced myself to roll out of bed, literally dragging myself out, putting on walking clothes and leaving with a cup of coffee.

I know how to look at things negatively, which leads to being anxious and depressed. It took a lot of practice to become an expert at being depressed and anxious. What do I mean by that? I recall very well my body and facial expressions when depressed or anxious. It took time to unlearn being depressed and to learn how to be joyous. By just changing my body and facial expression, I was halfway there. Have I achieved being the happiest person in the world every day of my life? Of course not, but I learned how to bounce back and be optimistic in many situations. I learned how to be proactive instead of reactive, not becoming a victim of circumstance but being in control of my emotions.

As with other mental conditions, triggers for depression can be biochemical—when it seems to take over my body out of the blue, or emotional—when recalling shameful, sad or hopeless events evokes deep sadness. It is said that depression often springs from thinking about the past while anxiety springs from playing in your head the worst possible outcomes of a situation.

How did my body respond to a depressed mind? I wanted to crawl into a ball on my bed and not move. When it was a mild depression, I still slouched, frowned or had a sad face accompanied by shallow breathing. I wanted to do nothing except dwell in misery. The world lost its appeal and colors. It was too much effort to do anything. Just trying to smile was huge, but it paid off. I was able to begin deep breathing, to cause oxygen to flow through my body. Then I would flex my fingers. That was better than nothing, right? I kept smiling, breathing, and moving fingers. Just staying in bed and smiling was a small step. I began to feel that cure was on the way. I read somewhere about a research where depressed subjects were asked to hold a pencil sideways in their mouths for a few minutes at a time. As a result of activating facial muscles that are used for smiling their mood elevated and depression lifted.

Fear: Friend or Foe?

Most of us are afraid of dying. It causes us to be fearful of accidents, catastrophes, and diseases. At times such fears paralyze us and begin to control our lives, as it happened to me on occasions when I was awaiting test results and battling health issues. Such fears prohibit us from living our lives to the fullest and reaching our God-given potential.

In many cases, experiencing fear is a good thing. Once a child learns that touching a hot or sharp object will hurt, they usually avoid doing that in the future. Being cautious is beneficial. But when does being vigilant become excessive? Where is the line that separates useful fears from becoming obsessive? We know that driving a car can lead to an accident. Does it keep us from ever getting behind a wheel? It did for one of my friends. She never learned to drive a car. Interestingly enough, she didn't have a problem being a passenger and that totally perplexed me, as one can become a victim of an accident regardless of being a driver or a passenger. When she lived in New York, with its extensive public transportation system, this was not an issue, but when her family moved to Southern California, she had to rely on her husband, children or friends to drive her. It became extremely inconvenient, but she never learned to drive.

One of our friends is afraid of flying. He took this fear to an extent that his family never took any vacations that required flying. Did he not hear that it is more likely for a person to die from a car accident than a plane crash?

At what point can fear become obsessive, interfering with the enjoyment of life? When is wearing a facial mask for protection from germs and viruses justifiable and when is it bizarre? Is it better to be open and trusting or extremely cautious and hostile toward strangers?

Do I need to trust my intuition when I sense something is not quite right? I heard a few stories about acting on hunches, which actually saved lives. But how justifiable is it to avoid flying or driving altogether because of fear? Shall we miss out on what this beautiful world has to offer because of our reservations? Is it right to always give in to fear? I don't have answers for others but I had to learn to overcome fears that affect my quality of living. They kept me from enjoying life to the fullest and I didn't like it.

I worked on my fear of flying and saw positive results. As an exercise, I imagined myself as a flight attendant or a pilot. I liked to imagine being a flight attendant who loved her job and I vividly imagined performing my duties as this attendant. I saw in my mind's eyes serving drinks, chatting with my coworkers, joking and laughing. Within a week of such practice my fear significantly diminished.

This can be applied to other fears. Sometimes fears can be overcome within an hour when the correct exercises are chosen and high levels of emotions are applied.

I met many people who were afraid of public speaking, but I remember one story in particular. As a little girl, Jane had to speak in public in a speech meet. She won her school competition and went on to the finals with another teammate. When they arrived at the other school, its unfamiliar surroundings scared her. She became paralyzed with fear. For years since this episode, Jane was afraid to speak in public. She tried, but it always made her feel extremely uncomfortable. A short while ago, when we met, she told me she was trying to fight this fear but it was extremely difficult. I shared with her a technique I learned that helped me tremendously: erasing and replacing memories. The idea is to imagine a particular episode that caused the emotional "hang up" and envision a different, happy scenario instead. Repeating it in your head over and over again will replace the old memory and help rid you of heavy emotional baggage.

I came across the following acronyms: FEAR: False Evidence Appearing Real as well as FEAR: Forget Everything And Run, or: Face Everything And Rise.

Facing My Fears

There were times when overpowering, debilitating fear gripped my whole being and I thought it would never leave. Fear seemed to take over my body and mind during a panic attack. When in the grips of it, I can feel nothing else. I hate even remembering those times—yikes! Everything around me was losing its appeal, even color. I felt as if I was losing my senses and my whole being was dissolving into a gray mush. Everything I enjoyed and held dear didn't matter anymore. It seemed all that was left was despair. Neither beautiful weather nor the things I normally enjoyed doing brought me any satisfaction or joy. I prayed for joy, I prayed for deliverance, but was not getting the results I so desperately longed for. I experienced miracles in my life before and was absolutely positive God would answer my prayers. Why was He so slow to act in this case? I was forlorn from hurt and weary from the darkness around me.

I tried doing everything possible to overcome fear step by step. I created a plan and then exposed myself to the fear triggers. I did it in small doses or imagined what I would do in certain situations, preparing myself. It was an incremental, continuous improvement. This method can be applied to many things, from overcoming fear to establishing a new habit, to learning a new language. Take one little step at a time, then it is not as scary and becomes possible. It really helps to approach any big obstacle or problem by dividing necessary actions into small steps.

Anxiety is a reaction of my body to stress or fear. The amygdala is the fear center of the brain. It is triggered when we are facing great challenge. Our natural reaction is to turn away from what stimulates our fears. Fear of ill health and death, financial disaster, confrontation, loneliness—any of these can paralyze us and take over our mind. I am trying to embrace my fears and face the symptoms of anxiety. It's okay to feel fear, acknowledge its presence in gratitude (it is designed to warn and protect me after all!) and to move forward, with caution if necessary.

Unveiling my deepest fears even to myself is scary in itself, but doing so I may get close to eventually uprooting it for good. I needed to acknowledge my fears and face them in order to eventually conquer them. I wanted to know where they came from, whether they are learned and developed from the experiences and observations of others.

Fighting Fear and the Urge to Control Things

It is a good idea to write fears down on pieces of paper and then burn them. I also can write my worst fears and triggers on a plate with a Sharpie, and then break it! Writing down my fears is helpful, especially separated into two categories: the reasonable and the unreasonable, which things I cannot control and which that I can. My upbringing pushed me into a victim mentality for quite some time, which in turn made me more fearful of possible negative outcomes. I became very good at focusing and dwelling on possible disasters instead of focusing on what I could control and change. I began asking questions: what are the things I can learn from any situation and challenge I face? Could it be that things were predestined and meant to happen in a certain way? How important is it to control things in my life? Can I make peace with the idea that I am unable to control everything and especially anyone? What is the worst possible outcome of a challenge at hand? What is the best possible scenario? After years of focusing on the worst, I finally began imagining the best, not the worst possible outcome.

Finally I realized this: if overwhelming fear is the overpowering force in my life, I can't experience the pure, exuberant joy I wholeheartedly seek. On the other hand, when I fill my heart with gratitude, there is no room for fear, it has to flee—fear and thanksgiving can't coexist in our heart. This is why gratitude brings me joy.

Processing Grief

Unexamined and unprocessed grief can resurface years later at the most inopportune moment, causing emotional turmoil and even physical pain. We need to allow reality to set in and to reflect. We should not try to ignore our feelings or try to move quickly away from these draining feelings. We often need to retrieve in solitude to process, examine and grieve. It came natural to me to block my strong negative emotions. I was uncomfortable and afraid to deal with them. When my father passed away, I was thrown off balance and tried everything to avoid feeling the devastation of this irreplaceable loss. But I did not know how to grieve. We all grieve in different ways, trying to make sense of unbearable loss.

There are ways to process emotions, letting them sink in for a while, to experience them fully right when the cause occurs, preventing them from haunting us later. For many it's very difficult not to dwell in beautiful memories with a person who died. Those memories wash over and then reality hits—the loved one is gone … when a very close and dear family member passes on, it seems impossible to process. Sometimes we need solitude and reflection; sometimes we need to voice our sorrows to a friend or someone who would listen with compassion, not just saying that it is going to be okay because they are uncomfortable with your raw grief. Psychologists and grief counselors are trained to help and guide us through the process.

Even if I viewed grief over the passing of a loved one as justifiable, the loss of a dream I saw as unjustifiable. I tried to block such thoughts even faster. Many different things can evoke feelings of loss and deep sadness. Now I know that regardless of how unjustifiable my emotions of sorrow (or even anger) may seem at first, I need to allow myself to fully feel and process them. Only later I learned to observe and analyze the cause and layers of sadness, feeling the pain fully before letting it go. Grieving and crying over the lost dream is okay. At times I needed the comfort of a few trustworthy friends to listen and pray with me, and also a quiet place to grieve alone. Now I allow myself to fall apart and grieve even over seemingly unimportant things, if they evoke strong emotions. I try to achieve a healthy balance of validating my emotions and eventually letting them go without holding on.

Chapter 10: Information Overload

Overthinking can drain your sanity, mental and physical energy, and time.

The issue is, we are all accountable for it. We have been told to end overthinking.

There is a massive disparity between creative thinking and overthinking. If you think creatively, you are not looking to downsize a decision. Instead, you are making a whole new decision overall.

Creative thinking indeed is helpful. It helps in building new ideas which can result in a positive outcome.

However, overthinking is not healthy. It makes our ideas stagnant.

So, here is what must know about overthinking and how it can destroy conversions.

Cognitive Bias

How people think, plays a vital role in overthinking.

From the way you have raised, lived as well as worked, all of us developed a cognitive bias.

So, meaning as a human being, we are geared towards doing or thinking things in a specific manner, and most of the time which can cloud our judgment.

Above are some of the many examples of passive biases which can twist our thinking process. Many famous conversion killers we have discovered include information and confirmation bias.

Confirmation Bias

Confirmation bias creeps wherever and all over. Usually, we look for information which justifies our very own preconceptions; or instead, we screw up details to fall in line.

Confirmation bias kills conversion, as we aren't always right. Regardless of the experiences you had before. Almost every market usually is different six months later.

There is an idea, which development is just an exceptional one. Like for instance, Airbnb grew, do you believe you could copy that in any business? Certainly not!

Since we had been successful some time ago, it doesn't mean we can idle by and do the same thing time again and again. Instead of being open-minded, it is simpler to prove to others, that, "maybe it will work yet again."

Information Bias

Due to the development of the internet, information bias is now easy to develop.

People take a data-driven method to decisions. They read far too many blogs. Most of the time, those blogs are not even relevant to what you are trying to obtain.

Sometimes, forty to seventy percent of the information required in making a choice is just enough. Spending a lot of time looking to rationalize edge-case scenarios can delay your decision. What is more, you also waste valuable time mentally testing thought, rather than putting it into action.

There is a similarity between information bias and information overload; however, in information overload, the issue is not searching for the information, but how much you have assimilated.

Seeking a lot of resources, seeking a lot of data burns you out. And if you are already exhausted, you aren't taking action. Thus, you are overload.

Come to think of it, and you have just put as one a development technique you have decided to do a bit further examination. You keep on reading, then suddenly, you are beginning to think more about whether or not what you have put jointly works.

You are taking in lots of information, and instead of carting off the key pieces, you are getting caught. Your developments and frontward momentum disappear.

Sad to say, most of the time, doing a lot is our biggest conversion destroyer, rather than trying structuring goals and breaking the whole thing down into more convenient milestones.

According to Seth Godin, "The cost of being wrong, is less than the cost of doing nothing."

If you are in doubt, be interested and test. You are destroying your conversion by doing nothing. You also are killing your conversion as you are trapped in information overload. All of these are not doing you any good.

Physical and Mental Symptoms Which Point Toward Information Overload

The whole thing should be done in moderation, including the assimilation of knowledge. Or else, it can seriously affect your physical and mental well-being in so many ways such as:

Increase your blood pressure

Low energy or mood

A significant decreased in cognitive performance that ultimately affects the skills in making a choice

Impaired vision

Finding it hard to focus

Strong pressure to check apps, voice mails, emails, etc

Diminished productivity

Vivid dreams

Insomnia

Tiredness

All these are symptoms that you are experiencing information overload.

What Should You Do to Keep Away from Information Overload?

Without a doubt, you are hungry and curious for information because accessing it anytime, and wherever is easy. No matter what idea comes into your mind, you want information about it and you check as a lot of resources as you can.

However, understanding the risks you expose yourself to, you must opt for solutions and techniques which will make sure a normal function of your brain.

Check the information

Just listen and read the information you think valuable for today. Choose information that can enhance your skills and knowledge. Or else, take for granted irrelevant information such as gossips, news, talk shows, and many others.

Choose Reliable Sources: It's always better to hear diverse opinions; however, more doesn't mean truer or better. Just pick the best sources.

Set a Limit

Is it really needed to read the news each morning or keep your posts updated daily on Twitter and Facebook? Set a time limit and avoid spending lots of time a day browsing social media sites or the news you read concerning your favorite Hollywood artist.

Prioritize Activities

There are some activities which are vital than others. Avoid overloading your schedule with lots of activities which need too much of your time and attention. Finish first the most vital one and if you have more time, do the next one.

Choose Conversations Smartly

A lot of people are able to leave you mentally or emotionally drained. Some might want to talk a lot and provide you lots of information as possible, while some will pass their concerns to you. Your energy and time are limited, therefore spend them smartly.

☐Learn How to Say No

If some projects are of your skill or knowledge, don't afraid or hesitate to say no. Additional work will decrease the quality and efficiency of your cognitive performance. In turn, this will not provide the outcomes you have been looking for.

☐Do What is Right

Yearly, there are a growing number of young people all over the world who died due to stroke. According to expert, one reason for this devastating fact is the overstimulation of their brain as they have a lot of responsibilities.

As a result, professionals recommend that you must re-energize your neuron and boost your resistance to damage by doing simple things like exercise, hydration, outdoor activities, and enough sleep.

Give More Time to Yourself

Spending time along can refresh your mind. So, take a break, and put all your thoughts and thinking into order by doing nothing, keep away from people, bad influences, and social media.

If you are experiencing the signs of information overload, what techniques do you apply to look for psychological balance?

Avoid Information Overload to End Overthinking!

The most actionable takeaways:

Give more of your time on getting things completed, concentrate on the action. Spend lots of your time in making progress and spend less time in negative thinking.

Break things down into easy to handle chunks

Overthink less and test more

Avoid reading too much, and do not look for too much information.

Be aware of why you're here, who you are, and where you are.

Knowing the Setback of Overthinking

As an individual, it is vital to understand the setback of obsessive thinking. It is also vital to know how to keep away from it. Most of the time, when we get in our heads, we get into problem. A new study conducted in the U.K involving 30,000 individuals revealed that giving so much time on negative things or events (specifically through self-blame and rumination) can be the most important predictor of today's most popular mental health issues.

Conquer Your Critical Inner Voice co-author, Dr. Lisa Firestone commented, 'time spent in thinking and reflection is constructive and optimistic- a rich setting for creativity and personal development. However, entering in our mind can also be harmful once we are unconstructively turned in opposition to ourselves. She also commented that there is a significant disparity between rumination and introspection. According to Dr. Lisa Firestone, introspection takes account of self-examination and healthy self-reflection. But rumination is like a brutal cycle of unconstructive thinking. It is discouraging and critical self-talk. Introspection can result in insights, self-understanding, solution, and goal setting. Rumination, however, can lead to self-doubting, makes you feel critical and stifled. This is also self-destructive.

In obsessive thinking, we engage in an unhelpful thought process which results in hostile results. We're listening to what Doctor Lisa refers to as a critical inner voice in our mind which sharpens in on the unconstructive factors of circumstances. This inner voice is like an aggressive coach, which feeds us a continuous flow of criticism and challenges and demoralizes our objectives. It is that thought which comes once we are about to go in various conditions like a job interview. You will fail this, and you are not capable of getting the position. Just like how worried you are. It is the conversation which plays in your mind evaluating your relationship: Why did she ignore more presence or why is she cold today? Perhaps I did or said something offending. She is losing interest. Perhaps she already finds someone else.

Therefore, why do people harbor this internal opponent which feed them awful advice and unconstructive commentary? The reality is that human beings are divided. We are divided between our anti-self and our real-self. Although our real-life is objective-directed, life-affirming as well as signifies our real desires and values, our anti-self is like an internal opponent that is self-critical, self, denying, doubtful and fearful, both towards us as well as towards others.

Keep in mind that real-self is developed from constructive experiences in life, healthy growth events, as well as traits and qualities we have seen in our loved ones and early caretakers. Anti-shelf is formed from our unconstructive experiences, damaging attitudes, and harmful occurrences we were encountered during our early lives. Like for instance, if you have a caretaker who sees you as no good, your inner voice tends to replicate this upsetting and cruel approach toward ourselves. As mature individuals, we are likely to self- parent, telling ourselves similar things we were told as kids. When you side with your anti-self and pay attention to your "critical inner voice," you can be led down a hurtful way which is not based on truth and reality. You might engage in an unhelpful flow of rumination, a kind of obsessive thinking which has been associated with stress, sadness as well as suicide.

It doesn't matter if you beat yourself up over a blunder you made in the past or worry about how you are going to succeed in the future, worrier is overwhelmed by anguishing thoughts- and their incapability to escape from you own head leaves you in a condition of continuous anguish.

While we think so much on a specific matter every now and then, some people cannot ever seem to settle down the continuous flows of thoughts. The inner monologue of these individuals takes account of two unhelpful and negative thought patterns- worrying and ruminating.

Screaming STOP or I Can't Take it Anymore

Will Not Help You!

If you can stop yourself from overthinking things, screams STOP, shatter a rubber band, set off a shock, then you would not be here. Sad to say, there is no off switch for overthinking. Screaming STOP is indeed the most innate reaction to overthinking. However, experts have found out that the effort to hinder some thoughts from consciousness results in an opposite and equal reply wherein the thoughts you are trying to hold back come swinging back with a revenge. Telling yourself to end thinking so much is like pressing on a ball under the water. Once you press harder, it pops higher. Thus, you aren't able to hold onto it.

Obsessed thinking an event, problem, or a conversation is a common way of dealing with anxiety. On the other hand, researches conducted by experts reveal that obsessed thinking and pondering is something worrying and stressful. It has a strong connection with stress, sadness, and depression. For a lot of people out there, overthinking a specific matter is only a habitual way of viewing the world surrounds them. But, that state of mind can result in extended periods of sadness. Research also reveals that can lead to some people to setback seeking medication. Knowing to deal with this kind of condition can help a person to set free of painful and hurtful occurrences in life and break out of damaging thought patterns.

Learn the Various Cognitive Distortions

Prior to starting to solve or cope with this condition, first and foremost, you will have to know what types of thoughts take place when you are engaging in this harmful activity. Any time you find yourself pandering to these unpleasant, painful, and self-doubting thoughts, you're on the way to obsessed thinking due to the cognitive distortions. Similarly, if you find yourself giving reasons to no carry-out something, or making reason and justification for your self-doubt. Most popular cognitive distortions take account of the following:

All or nothing thoughts: you believe in things which are absolute and viewing each condition as being black or white.

Overgeneralization: viewing one unconstructive occurrence as a constant flow of embarrassment or defeat.

Mental filtering: just settling on unconstructive things which include results, feeling as well as thoughts, while taking for granted all the optimistic and helpful factors of those scenarios or situations.

Discounting the optimistic: believing that no one in your admirable features or achievements matter.

Jumping to conclusions: either supposing that others are thinking/ responding unconstructively towards you without any proof (this also known as mind-reading) or believing that an incident will be worse without any proof for this conclusion.

Emotional reasoning: this signifies believing that how you feel mirrors a truth about yourself.

Minimization or magnification: this refers to blowing unconstructive things out of proportion or minimizing the value of good deeds.

"Should" declarations: this refers to punishing yourself for things which should and should not be done and said.

Labeling: this refers to turning shortcomings or mistakes into a feature attribute of yourself. Like for instance, turning the idea "I was wrong" into "I am a failure, or I am a loser."

Blame and personalization: this refers to internalizing mistake for cases or occurrences you are not liable for or blaming someone for events and situations which they had no control over.

See How You Overthink

There are many avenues for a person to overthink everything; some of these are because of cognitive distortions. Catastrophizing is one kind of overthinking. This thought pattern takes place anytime you instantly foresee an unconstructive result in some occurrence or series of occurrences and jump to the conclusion that such a result would be unbearable or devastating. This thought pattern is a mixture of overgeneralizing things and jumping straight to the conclusion.

Trying to know the specific cognitive distortions that affect your overthinking is very important. Put down the thoughts you suffer, and try to categorize which ones could fall into the classification of cognitive distortions.

You need to practice learning to distinguish your overthinking thoughts as they come up. By simply labeling your thoughts once you become sensitive to them might help a lot. Try silently uttering the word "thinking" as you start to overthink, might help you in grounding as well as breaking out the increasing thought pattern.

Always Pay Close Attention to your Feeling Falling into autopilot type during the period of your day is easy. On the other hand, once your time or day is filled with events which can encourage stress and depression, you might be walking blindly into an event which will lead you to think so much and catastrophize.

Try to Command A Personal "Check-In"

Evaluate how you are feeling as you come into different situations and scenario which are likely to induce the pattern of overthinking.

Determine any case in point in which you start to pander to patterns of thinking so much. You have to avoid judging yourself from it, appreciate it prior to working to alter it.

Challenge Automatic Thoughts

If you have recognized an event of catastrophizing or overthinking, now you can start to dispute the legality of those feelings and beliefs. Challenging the thoughts by means of remembering that feelings and beliefs aren't facts might help you escape from the pattern of overthinking.

Feelings and beliefs aren't always a sign of actuality and authenticity. Most of the time, these thoughts are uninformed, warped, or just wrong. By allowing setting a reliable insight of perception of beliefs free, you will be more able to consider other potentials. Or accept that overthinking is not always right.

Look at what real, objective proof you have to back the cognitive distortions and overthinking patterns which you are experiencing. There's a good possibility that you'll not be capable of coming up with real, compelling proof that the beliefs and feelings you are experiencing right now have any grounds inaccuracy.

Silently trying to say, "These are only thoughts, and these aren't real." Saying this mantra over and over again might help a lot in disengaging from the increasing thought patterns you are stuck in.

Substitute and Swap these Cognitive Distortions with Genuine Facts

Once the pattern of overthinking is increasingly becoming out of your control, you may feel it so hard to get away that thought pattern. On the other hand, if you know how to determine what thoughts you are experiencing right now are not real, then you can fairly and easily swap that pattern of thought with a more realistic and truthful one. Try to say this thing to yourself, "If I admit that my theories and overthinking aren't basis in facts, then what are the truths in this case?"

Although a condition ended defectively and imperfectly, you can give more of your time on what to carry out another way in the future as an option to dwelling on what you must have done or said in the past. At first, it will not easily come. On the other hand, if you retrain your mind to process events in another way, sooner or later everything will be easier for you.

Try to Ask Friends or Loved Ones Who Are Receptive to the Condition for their Participation or Input

At times asking a trusted colleague, relative or a friend whether you are overthinking or overreacting to everything can help in realizing that there is no reason for you to keep on thinking that way.

Positive Self-Talk Can Replace Overthinking and Self-Doubt

How you talk to yourself has an impact on your feeling. So, rather than criticizing yourself or pondering on bad feelings, try to spend your time on the things you excel. Are you good at writing? Do you love singing and dancing? Give more of your time to the things that make you happy. This will not just help you get away from ruminating bad things.

Chapter 11: Symptoms Of Negativity

Now, we are on to discussing some signs that indicate the presence of negative energy.

1. When you find yourself complaining about things more than you should.

In life, different situations provoke our emotions more than some others do. Pay attention to those situation, relationships or responsibility that make you complain and become a nag. It is not healthy for you. You should get out such designs or construct before it makes you into what you are not.

You'll see that overtime, with consistent complaints, your positive, optimistic stand view will begin to get shaky and eventually, will fade out, to give room for negativity. Simply put, complaints drain our positive energy and replace it with negativity.

2. The frequent feeling of being on the edge, or being angry.

When anger becomes a persistent emotion, it becomes detrimental to our physical and mental health. You should avoid situations and events that get you to the edge too often. To do this, you have to grow in emotional intelligence and become more emotionally aware.

3. Feelings of anxiety and or depression

Feelings of anxiety and depression are among the most two commonly reported symptoms in the world. Physicians are seen by people suffering from anxiety and depression more than all other illnesses combined. Constantly feeling anxious or depressed is a force of negative energy that needs to be addressed.

4. Loss of interest in interactions

Whenever you notice that it is getting difficult and more difficult to engage in interactions with people, then there is a problem. To combat this, you have to practice and listen more.

5. Increasingly becoming more and more sad

Negativity as you already know, will only bring your focus to the negatives of life. The more you zoom in on the bad sides of the people around you, or even yourself, you'll begin to criticize so much that you'll become a sad soul. As with so many other forms of negative energy, criticism has a multiplying effect.

6. When you prefer your lone moments to meeting people

You want to know a negative person? well he is someone who prefers to be on his own and not with people, because he thinks everyone he meets is trash and no-good for him. I know a lot of us can be like this, but it becomes a problem when it is on the extreme level. While some alone time is healthy, it's not healthy to experience a sudden desire for seclusion.

Chapter 12: Planning & Organizing Your

Day To Simplify Your Life

Now let's take what we have learned so far and put it all together into an action plan. We will have several levels and you will be able to choose what you would like to start on first. You may find you want to handle multiple issues at once or take them one at a time. There is no one way to work the program.

For the purpose of illustration, I am going to use our newly divorced mother of two children and follow her through this exercise of creating an action plan.

Pull together all of your exercises and notes. In your notebook, turn to a new page and set up the following information. What we are going to do is go through each of the exercises and list them with the rank from the Core Values Exercise. We will fill in information from each of the exercises and see what picture begins to form.

List of Problems to be Addressed					
Problem Areas	Ra nk	Issu e	Loo p?	Emoti on	Possib le Soluti on
Home Environ ment	5	Can' t kee p up wit h hou se or yar d wor k.	y	anger	Set up a sched ule with kids.

Background survey

The answers you gave here are going to help us prioritize your action plan and may give us some insight into helping to shut down the loops.

The goal for a life well lived: See her two children through college and on to a career they enjoy.

Secret Passion: Enjoys painting/drawing. Wanted to be an illustrator. She is a director in the marketing department of a manufacturing company.

Hint for managing self effectively: Set hard deadlines but keep the mood light.

Missing from life: Personal time.

Qualities that inspire: Not losing sight of the bigger picture. Able to stay calm when being directly challenged or criticized.

Roadblocks to goals: Overcommitting.

How to get back on track: Forgive and start again as if I did not fall off.

Regular exercise: Dog walk in the evening.

Physician: Yes.

List medical issues: 40 lbs. overweight, not enough exercise.

Core Values Survey

The core values list is also part of the prioritizing process. I want you to use the items that are scored 1 through 6 in your action plan. Anything 7 or higher does not need our attention at the moment.

Physical Environment - Work (7) - not much we can change, but it is a quiet work environment, with working equipment and up-to-date software.

Physical Environment - Home (5) - I can't seem to keep up with everything. I'm doing well to get the clothes washed and folded, and dinner cleaned up. The main rooms get vacuumed regularly, but the other rooms only once or twice a month. And I never have time for yard work, since the divorce. I can't even think about painting or replacing anything right now while the kids are still in grade school.

Career - (8) - I'm lucky to get to work in my field of choice, and it is a good company for working mothers.

Health & Diet - (5) - Doc says I'm 40 lbs. overweight. I think I eat well, just too much.

Friends & Family - Friends (8) - I have several circles of friends: parents from the children's school/events, some from college, and some from work. Although, again, since the divorce, my time has been limited and I don't see them very often.Maybe it used to be an eight.

Friends & Family - Family (6) - Quite a bit of our family is still in this area, and when I first started dating seriously and graduated from college, I had to set some boundaries for my own free time. Maybe that number should be higher; I'm actually seeing more of both sides since the divorce.

Religion & Spirituality - (8) - for both. I keep the kids close to nature and their father and his family shares their religion.

Personal Time - (2) - The only time I have to myself is getting ready for bed, sleeping and getting up in the morning.

Income - (8) - It's tighter now that we have two households, but we are okay.

Recreation & Exercise - (5) - Again, time is tight with all of the children's events. I don't have much time for my exercise - those are some of the friends I've been missing. I haven't even thought about vacation, given all the changes.

Worry Loop

Take a look at your worry loop exercise. In this example, it looks like our over-thinker may be more upset with her parent's than she is with her sister. Either way, what she wants is out of her control.

The Worry	Why	Action	Outcome
Why can't my sister hold a steady job?	She has three kids to take care of and she lives with our parents.	Have set her up with jobs and job interviews.	She always ends up leaving the job after about

			six-nine months.
How can help her find a job she will keep?	I want her to be happy, but responsible	Talked to her about getting some career counseling	Ended up in a fight, again.
Why won't she act like an adult?	Drives me crazy that our parents let her off the hook.	Talked to my parents, but they make excuses for her	I got mad and stormed out.

The Worry	Why	Action	Outcome
Annual Spring	Not sure what to wear	May just let the kids go with my	None yet

156

Pool Party	this year.	sister or the grandparents and skip it.	
I don't feel good about the way I look	Gained weight with divorce	Tried dieting, without much success	Still fat - duh
Don't want to be seen.	Ran into an ex with a new girlfriend and she looks great.	None stay home.	Stress eating.

Mean-Mouth Loop

Take a look at your Mean-Mouth issues, if you have any. Our mother of two seems to have come up with another family issue from when she was young.

The Mean Talk	Who was this?	Action	Outcome
Are you going to feel comfortable in that outfit	Mom always questioned my outfits - I was a bit overweight as a child. Grew out of it in middle school.	If I wrote her a letter, I would let her know her questioning me ruined my whole day. I spent the entire day worried about how I looked.	My ex started snipping at me when I gained weight before the divorce.

			Now I understand why it bothered me so much. I'm back in grade school.

Emotional Triggers

Again, we are starting to see some overlap of anxieties. Add the issues from fear, anger, sadness, and guilt to the action plan under the Problem Areas.

Emotional Triggers	
Interest	**Joy**
music, dance	jumping in the pool
learning new skills	listening to music
swimming	hiking
reading	Seeing my kids learn - the moment when they "get"

	something.
cooking	
Fear	**Sadness**
sick or injured children	misunderstandings from the past
getting sick or injured me	loss of a family member, including pets
not being able to care for family	not being able to help someone
not finding a new partner - thought I would be married forever	
Love	**Comfort**
old friends	kids in bed asleep
laughing kids	the scent of flowers in the yard
stroll through the garden	cat purring
canoeing	finishing a project

Anger *	Guilt*
Laziness	betrayal of trust
not taking care of family	deceiving family or friends
not being about to discuss something rationally	not being able to save my marriage
free-loading	
*Self-Medicating	

Listing Worries

Type of Worrier: Passive-Aggressive Worrier	Over-thinking Loop	Efficiency Problem	Sharing Opportunity	Possible Solutions
Unexpected bills	x			List - Payment schedule/credit card
Repairs on		x		List -

kitchen				prioritize - schedule
No time for yard	x		x	Kids are old enough to help now
Lose weight for summer	x			what are you eating
Organize hobby/work/home	x			List and schedule
Dogs need bath			x	teach oldest to bath small dogs
The kitchen sink is			x	end of meal routine -

always full of dirty dishes				3 weeks
House needs a thorough cleaning	x			family meeting - ask for help
Kids aren't using hamper for dirty clothes			x	family meeting - other routines
Wet towels in the hamper			x	family meeting - tired of repeating myself
Work out children's savings account with Ex	x			Make an agenda similar to a work meeting - stick to

				it.

Analysis Loop

	Analysis Loop - Why are you looping through this particular discussion?
Who:	Ex-Husband
What:	The argument last year when you asked if he was having an affair. You wanted to set up counseling. You had no idea that the marriage was over in his head.
Outcome:	He moved out that same night - to girlfriend's house.
Feelings:	Devastated, anger, hurt, stupid, clueless
Desired Outcome:	You thought it was just a rough patch. How could you get so out of touch with your own husband?

Compiling Your Fix List

Well, here it is. You have assembled your fix list of issues that are making you crazy as they loop through your head undermining your confidence. Now we need to breakdown the Possible Solutions column to see where we need to add help. On our example mom's emotional trigger list, she indicated that anger and guilt could trigger self-medicating, so I'm going to put an asterisk next to those emotions.

Fix List					
Problem Areas	Rank	Issue	Loop?	Emotion	Possible Solution
Home Environment	5	Can't keep up with house or yard work.	y	anger *	Set up a schedule with kids.
worry list		Unexpected Bills.	y	fear	Put the due dates

					of all recurring bills in your calendar; try to use a credit card for emergencies only.
worry list		Repairs on the kitchen.			List what needs to be repaired, prioritize, and

				sched ule.
worry list		No time for the yard.	y	anger *	Set up a sched ule with kids.
worry list		Organize hobby/w orkspace s at home.	y	anger *	List what needs organi zing and sched ule one night a week to work on.
worry		Dogs			Teach

list		need a bath.			kids how to bath dogs.
worry list		The kitchen sink is always full of dirty dishes.			Start-end of meal routine.
worry list		House needs a thorough cleaning.			Start cleaning routine. Put various chores on the schedule.

worry list		Kids aren't using hamper for dirty clothes.			Family meeting - develop new habits together.
worry list		Wet towels being put in the hamper.			Family meeting - develop new habits together.
Health & Diet	5	40 lbs. overweight.	y	fear	Work on a health

					y meal plan.
worry loop		Weight gain is causing a worry loop.	y	anger *	Meal plan.
worry loop		Lose weight for summer.	y	sham e	Meal plan.
Famil y	6	Feelings that younger sister is taking advantag e of parents is part of worry loop.	y	anger *	Need to let go.

worry loop		Mad at parents for enabling irresponsible behavior, also worry loop.	y	anger *	Need to let go.
		Boundaries have been an issue in the past.			Something to remember.
mean-mouth		Mom made her feel self-conscience about weight and clothes when she	y	anger */sad	Need to let go.

		was in grade school.			
		Sickness or injury of family members or self.		fear	Write down instructions for emergency or death. That is all you can control.
trigger		Not being able to care for the family.		fear	Learn to avoid trigger

		Never finding a new husband.		fear/ anger *	Increase social functions.
trigger		Laziness, free-loading.	y	anger *	Learn to avoid trigger
trigger		Not being able to discuss something rationally.	y	anger *	Learn to avoid trigger
worry list		Work on children's savings accounts with Ex.			Schedule meeting with ex

					and have an agenda ready.
analysis loop		You keep playing the conversation the night your husband left you over and over in your head.	y	anger *	Need to let go.
Personal Time	2	Has no personal time.			Getting help from kids

					will help free up some time.
trigger		A misunderstanding from the past.		sadness	Learn to avoid trigger
trigger		Loss of family member.		sadness	Learn to avoid trigger
trigger		Not being able to help someone.		sadness	Learn to avoid trigger
trigger		Betrayal of trust.		guilt*	Learn to

					avoid trigger
trigger		deceiving family or friends		guilt*	Learn to avoid trigger
trigger		not being able to save a marriage		guilt*	Learn to avoid trigger
Rec & Exercise	5	Stress eating as a result of divorce has resulted in weight gain and is making	y	anger*	Take some of the time you are freeing up and work

		you unhappy.			in more time for exerci se.
		With so many activities schedule with kids, not the time for an exercise routine.			Figure out what kind of exerci se you want to do.

Feel Good Emotions

You have put in your emotional triggers for your loops so you can start planning actions to shut them down. Now let's use some of the positive triggers you indicated and set those against the negative triggers. For example:

When anger is triggered distract yourself with something from the interest column - read a book, listen to music.

If you are overcome with sadness, look at your joy triggers or comfort triggers and take ten minutes to experience those emotions

Make sure your work areas at home and at work have reminders of these positive triggers. You have only to glance over at a picture of your kids (two-legged or four-legged) to bring a smile to your face at times of stress.

Don't forget your positive affirmations. You are confident that you can succeed and reach your goals!

Congratulations!

You have assembled a list of issues that have been stopping you from enjoying your life in some fashion. Now let's work on the best way to handle the issues. Using our example list we are going to drill down another level.

Home Environment is more a matter of setting up some house rules and reinforcing them until the solutions become a habit for family members.

Health & Diet is going to take some meal planning, will power, and a closer look at current eating habits.

Family is full of emotional issues. Not much here that we can set and forget with our calendar. You can get your affairs in order and write up instructions for a lawyer in case of death or disability. And the meeting with your ex concerning the children's savings can be scheduled. The rest of this is going to need more work.

Personal Time shows the listing of many triggers. This may mean that you are holding all these feelings in and not dealing with them. This is another area for more work before we put it on the action plan.

Recreation & Exercise has emotional aspects tied to the items concerning the divorce. But I think with some work and help from family this can be resolved with scheduling and some discipline when it comes to exercise.

All Aboard!

Knock out what you can right away. Pick a convenient time to have a family meeting and set your agenda.

Kids will rotate setting and clearing the table each week. Clearing includes rinsing dishes and putting them in the dishwasher.

Everyone will rinse dishes and put them in the dishwasher after use. No stacking in the sink.

Wet towels must be dried prior to dropping in hamper.

As soon as you change, put your dirty clothes in the hamper.

Volunteer needed to make reminder signs to post over hamper, in rooms, and at the kitchen sink.

Will meet again in three weeks to see how changes are progressing.

Our example mom realizes while she is waiting to get kids from the practice, she can come twenty minutes early and get some walking in or work on the park equipment. This will give her two 20 minute workout sessions a week in addition to the dog walks. She will also be increasing the length of the dog walks to add more steps to her day.

In the set it and forget it column our mom schedules an appointment with a family lawyer to get a will set up. And she schedules the meeting with her ex to talk about the savings account for the children. Our mom has also done some reading up on the Mediterranean Diet and has scheduled some time to sit down and figure out meals and when she can cook. Some evenings are too full to make dinner from scratch. She needs to have something ready to go. This will cut down of fast food stops and pizza orders. Her calendar looks something like this. And because she has the kids helping with more chores, she can make better use of some personal time. When the children are with their father every other weekend, she sees she has time to work on other projects or maybe schedule time with a friend to go to a movie.

Already we should have some relaxing of the shoulders and be able to release some of the stress that that was being held in the body due to lack of action.

Sunday	Monday	Tuesday	Wednesday	Thursday	Friday	Saturday
			7:00 Family Meeting	Walk during swim practice 5;00	w/ dad *	Meal Planning, Shopping - w/dad*

w/ dad		Walk during ball practice 5;00		Walk during swim practice 5;00		Kids Game 10:00 in town
	Meet with family lawyer 3:30	Walk during ball practice 5;00		Walk during swim practice 5;00	w/ dad *	Swim meet 6:30 a.m. out of town, w/dad (Get den

						clea red for craft roo m org) *
w/ dad		Wal k duri ng ball pra ctic e 5;0 0	7:00 Famil y Meeti ng	Wal k duri ng swi m prac tice 5;00		Mee t with Ex 1:30
		Wal k duri ng ball pra		Wal k duri ng swi m		

		ctice 5;00		practice 5;00		

Time to Dig

Now we need to figure out what to do with the issues that you can't put on the calendar. There were quite of few issues in the area of Family and Personal that needs to be addressed. It looks like they may be intertwined, but don't jump to conclusions. There are definite issues with the sister and how it appears the parents are enabling her by letting her and her children live at their house.

She has also mentioned being upset with her mother for making her feel self-conscious about her body image. Who knows, that might also be tied up with the sister in some way.

For your emotional items that cannot be scheduled like the examples above. Start with your journal. Write down what you meant by the statements you see on your

Fix List. Drill down a bit further by using the Analysis Loop exercise. Use the letter-writing method to let your side of the story is heard once and for all.

Connect the Dots

Look for connections to triggers. In our example, I see where laziness and free-loading are listed as an anger trigger under family. Again this points strongly to the sister, but do those thoughts pop up when our mom journals about the situation with her sister? They might or it may be that this is a completely different issue perhaps with the husband or something from her past. When you identify triggers in your writing. Use a highlighter and mark those so they stand out. Then think about what you have written. There is probably a hint as to how to avoid that trigger in the writing.

If after several weeks of working with your journal and sifting through your thoughts and memories, you haven't managed to stop certain loops. It might be time to think about scheduling an appointment with a counselor. With all the work you have already completed, you and your counselor should be able to get the situation figured out fairly quickly.

Liquid Courage?

Think about the past several weeks, when have you reached for a drink or other substance to numb the pain? The emotions anger and guilt were the two that our example mom indicated might trigger her to self-medicate. Be honest and keep a log of the days and time of day you are triggered to reach for a drink or pill to help you cope. Put it down on the calendar with the rest of the items and see if there is a pattern that you may have been unaware of or ignoring.

Perhaps our mom finds that she doesn't have alcohol too excess that often, every other week or so. But when she charts it, she realizes that it's the Friday and Saturday night that the children are over at their dad's house. So, some of her built-in personal time is being self-sabotaged by alcohol. That sheds new light on the way she might view some of her issues under personal time.

~ When you do things in the present that you can see, you are shaping the future that you are yet to see. ~

- Idowu Koyenikan, Wealth for All: Living a Life of Success at the Edge of Your Ability Pulling Everything Together

Set your Fix List and your Calendar side by side. Look at them closely and create your action plan. Your action plan should have enough detail to achieve a very specific goal. You also want to keep in mind a way to measure the achievement of goals and accountability. You might post on Facebook to friends that you are training for a certain walk/run. Let their interest and excitement feed yours and visa-versa.

Write out what you are going to do the next three weeks to put everything you have learned and practiced into work. Be very specific with times and dates and places when you can.

If you need a daily action plan when you first start out, make one. Most people do well with the three-week layout so that they don't feel like they are micromanaging themselves. A quick to-do list makes a good daily action plan.

Example:

Action Plan

Every third Wednesday, starting this week, we will have a family meeting to go over issues or concerns with the goal of making the house run smoother. In this first meeting, I will set down some ground rules, hand rising, and no interruptions when someone is talking. I will install a whiteboard which will have the main topic of the meeting which in this case is dirty dishes and dirty clothes/towels. I will also ask the kids if they have issues they would like to discuss. Then we'll go from there and see what happens for the next three weeks.

To increase my exercise I will arrive early to pick up the kids and plan to walk from 5:00 to 5:30 while the kids are at practice.

I am also going to invite other parents to join me. I will also increase the dog walks from 10 minutes to 20 minutes.

I am meeting with the lawyer in two weeks to find out what I need to do to safeguard the children's future.

I am meeting with my ex-husband in four weeks to resolve how we are going to handle the children's college fund.

I have an annual check-up scheduled in two months, so I don't feel a need to schedule an appointment any sooner.

My goal is to have lost 10 pounds by the annual check-up.

I have set up a time for meal planning this Saturday and plan to do some research on high-protein, low-carb diets.

I will review my fix list in three weeks prior to our next family meeting to determine what needs to be added or adjusted.

For the time being, I am journaling my loops and when I feel triggers set off overthinking bouts. It is actually getting easier to control some of them.

I may need to speak to my physician to find a counselor for this situation with my sister. That worry is in my head quite a bit and I can't seem to let go of it.

Overall, I am feeling less stress and more hopeful that I can get through this hard time.

Conclusion

Wayne Gretzky once said, "You lose a hundred percent of the shots you don't take". Time is sometimes a luxury that you can't afford, and overthinking is a waste of our precious time. If you find yourself ruminating, experiencing an above-normal amount of fear and anxiety, and your thinking does not lead to inspired action, you are overthinking. In the short-term, overthinking can lead to anxiety, fear, and a lack of self-confidence. In the long-term, research has shown that overthinking can lead to dreaded ailments like high blood pressure, hypertension and, in worse cases, even death.

However, rational and critical thinking are essential, especially as all action or inaction has consequences, be they negative or positive. If you channel the energy that you spend while overthinking into action, you will be sure to achieve the results that you desire, if not immediately, then over the course of time and trial and error. In some cases, it may be better to risk making a mistake than to risk the result of inaction, but this is only to be advised when your potential errors can be reversed and do not lead to a loss of time or material resources.

Aside from the fact that taking action saves you from the mental stress of overthinking, it also channels your energy into something that will be more productive and rewarding for you. There are many different types of decision-making that you can use to make decisions; choose the one that works best for you and stick with it. There is no hard-and-fast rule for the amount of time that you should spend considering all possible scenarios before taking action. It is less about the amount of time that you spend and more about whether your thinking process remains logical and productive.

It is especially important to avoid overthinking in life or death situations. For example, a renowned brain surgeon, Dr. Ben Carson, was once was faced with a dire situation where he had to act quickly to save an accident victim, even though he was only a new resident doctor. However, despite the risk involved, he understood the importance of quickly deciding on a course of action; Dr. Ben Carson carried out the operation, and it was a successful one, thus marking the beginning of an illustrious career as a renowned brain surgeon. Had he been prone to overthinking, the patient would most certainly have died.

Even when the consequences of overthinking are much less dire, so many dreams remain dreams because the individuals with creative ideas and brilliant imaginations are too fearful or anxious from overthinking to put their dreams into practice. Without action, a work of art as tangible and beautiful as the world-famous Mona Lisa painting would not exist. History will forever celebrate people like Leonardo da Vinci for their countless contributions to the arts; they will also celebrate inventors like Paul Darwin or Michael Faraday. These individuals achieved great things through inspired action, not overthinking.

Action is necessary to put our most inspired thoughts and ideas into practice, to solve problems and resolve issues, and to live our productively and fully. Overthinking paralyzes us, preventing us from taking the very actions that will ensure our contentment, fulfilment, and survival. By overcoming overthinking and learning how to incorporate rational, critical thinking in our lives, we can put our most inspired ideas into action and leave a lasting mark on the world.